HEART TUNING

HEART TUNING

A GUIDE TO BETTER FAMILY WORSHIP

JOHN & MILLIE
YOUNGBERG

REVIEW AND HERALD PUBLISHING ASSOCIATION
Washington, DC 20039-0555
Hagerstown, MD 21740

This book was
Edited by Gerald Wheeler
Designed by Richard Steadham
Type set: 11/12 Palatino

PRINTED IN U.S.A.

Library of Congress Cataloging in Publication Data

Youngberg, John, 1932-
Heart-tuning.

1. Seventh-day Adventists—Doctrines. 2. Family—Religious life. I. Youngberg, Millie, 1926-
II. Title.
BX6154.Y68 1985 249 85-14391
ISBN 0-8280-0284-3

Contents

Introduction

Distinctives of Seventh-day Adventist Family Life

Is the Adventist message for the family a carbon copy of what hundreds of other Christian churches are teaching about marriage, communication, and the home—or do we have a unique and distinctive insight and approach for today's family? A careful analysis reveals that conservative Christians do have a common core of family principles derived from the Bible that sets them apart from the secular and humanistic marriage and family guidelines that characterize twentieth-century culture.

Though we enthusiastically support the wealth of helpful family resources streaming from our fellow Christian communions and realize that secular research in sociology is also contributing helpful insights, we believe Seventh-day Adventism has two unique perspectives. These, together with the great basics of the gospel, constitute our raison d'être—the reason for our existence—and our distinct contribution to the family life movement.

First, the heart-tuning and restoration of family relationships and God-family relationships is prophetic and must be fulfilled before the coming of the great and terrible day of the Lord. God is giving in the spirit and power of Elijah a final heart-turning and heart-tuning call designed to lead our generation toward Him, and family members toward one another. As Satan wars unceasingly against marriage and the family, God purposes before His second coming in a final display of His power to " 'restore all things' " (Mark 9:12, R.S.V.)—including the twin Edenic institutions of marriage and the day of the family. (The Sabbath and the family belong together.) Through His last warning message God calls the world back to the Ten Commandments, which establish the believer's true hierarchy of values: God first (commandments 1-4), family next (5), then others (6-9), and things last (10). Before asking His people to follow this lifestyle, God first presents Himself as the Redeemer who has already freed them from bondage (see Ex. 20:2). This proclamation, which we commonly refer to as the Elijah message, prepares the earthly family to accept its privilege of uniting with the heavenly one.

The second distinctive is the emphasis placed on the morning and evening family altar. Adventism sees family worship in five dimensions: as *adoration;* as *covenant renewal;* as *sacrifice*—where the merits of Christ's sacrifice on the cross are claimed and constitute the family's victory over the enemy; as *instruction* so that the family may teach and hand on its religious heritage to the next generation; and as a *celebration* of familyness. Seen in this broad perspective, family worship produces the forum for all kinds of good things to happen in the family. It creates an opportunity for spiritual nurture to take place and sets the family apart as sealed and protected in the blood of the Lamb.

The basic issue of the last days will be worship. Those who obey the final call of the three angels, Scripture identifies as those who worship Him who made heaven and earth (Rev. 14:7), whereas those who are lost are identified as those who render homage to an apostate power.

Placing the "blood on the doorposts" by morning and evening worship consists of much more than just setting aside ten minutes twice a day. It involves more than externalizing. The heaping together of twelve stones did not capture the essence of worship in olden times. It was the internalizing of the meaning of the vicarious sacrifice that constituted it as worship.

Families whose worship is not a vibrant, covenant-renewing experience need to examine their lifestyle. An absent or ineffective family worship may be the symptom of a bigger difficulty. Perhaps it represents a sharing of stale shewbread rather than warm loaves fresh from our personal communion with God. Perhaps the fire of the Holy Spirit on the altar has gone out. If worship isn't "working," it requires that we take a long look at our way of life, our priorities, and the pace of our existence. In some cases it may demand major surgery such as moving out of the cities, changing jobs, and reordering commitments. But if we permit true personal and family worship to become the measuring rods of our lives, they will not cease their work until they have brought our whole lifestyle into harmony with the will of God, until our hearts are in tune with God and one another.

The family may use this book during its worship. You can give its members assignments from the worship activities at the end of the chapters. By a little research or preparation you can thus encourage everyone to become involved and make his/her contribution to a positive family relationship at the worship hour.

John and Millie Youngberg

The Protecting Hedge

"Fathers and mothers, however pressing your business, do not fail to gather your family around God's altar. Ask for the guardianship of holy angels in your home."—Child Guidance, *p. 520.*

Five hundred feet whizzed by Sandy as though she sped past them on a toboggan run. The glacier-polished slope of the Tuolumne River was as slick as ice. Now the deafening roar of Le Conte Falls thundered in her ears. How could she stop her Evel Knievel type of ride before plunging over the edge of the falls? All the river offered to grab hold of was green algae, itself clinging to the slimy rocks. Was the day that had begun with such happiness to end in death from her accidental "waterboggan" ride?

That morning the family had gathered around the campfire before continuing their backpacking trip into Yosemite National Park's high country. The blended voices of father, mother, and six children had sung:

"Father, we thank Thee for the night,
and for the pleasant morning light;
For rest, and food, and loving care,
and all that makes the day so fair.
Help us to do the things we should,
to be to others kind and good;
In all we do, at work or play,
to love Thee better day by day."

As the last notes died away into the forest, the father petitioned God for His loving care to place the family into the hands of protecting angels that day. And then they started working their way around a two-thousand-foot stretch of waterfalls, packs bulging with twelve days' provisions.

Ten-year-old Sandy liked the outdoors. God seemed so close. One thing she couldn't endure was being left behind. "Wait up!" she cried. But Dad, who had problems of his own to think about, didn't hear. He had to get to their next campsite. Before dark, they needed to set up camp, eat supper, and hoist the food high between some trees in bear bags to prevent unwelcome visitors that night.

"Wait up!" she cried again. Her eyes filled with tears. She wanted to catch up with her dad. She lunged forward along the rocky ledge, but her rapid movement caused the weight of the backpack to shift and her body veered toward the precipice on her right. "Oh, no!" she panicked. "I'm about to fall!" As she teetered on the edge, it seemed that an invisible hand pushed on her heavy pack. The weight shifted to the left, and she regained her footing on the precarious ridge.

When Sandy arrived at the campsite she unbuckled the backpack, changed into her swimming suit, and went to the river to take a slide in the fast-moving water. At first she squealed with glee as she slipped along. She planned to go only a little way in the shallow part. However, the granite river bottom sloped more than she thought, suddenly whipping her into the current. Faster and faster she whizzed by the big rocks and boulders on the edge of the swift-moving stream. The slimy green algae gave her nothing she could grasp. If only she could catch a limb or straddle a rock. "Jesus, help me!" she cried. Although Sandy tried desperately, she could not stop her plunge. Fear gripped her heart as the current hurdled her down the final stretch toward the falls.

Seventeen-year-old Charlene, hiking up the trail, arrived at the falls just in time to see the rushing water push Sandy to the brink. She saw her enter the two-stepped cascade from which the water fell free to jagged rocks below. In a split second the roaring falls would swallow its prey. And then Charlene saw the miracle. Right before her eyes an invisible hand pushed Sandy back. In a moment it thrust her back up the falls against the current, where she latched onto a rock, straddling it with her legs. In a frightened daze, Sandy lifted herself onto the rock and then stumbled to a large flat boulder where she collapsed, trembling and totally exhausted. Screaming, Charlene ran up the path to get her father. Rushing down the rocky terrain, he spied his daughter lying motionless on the boulder, unable to speak. Then she began to sob. After comforting her, Sandy's physician father examined her and found that she didn't have a scratch or a bruise on her body.

That evening after supper, the campers hoisted their provisions by a wire high between two trees, well out of the reach of hungry bears. About two hundred pounds of food reached its position as Charlene and Pam watched from below. Suddenly—snap! A grommet anchor for the wire gave way, and the bear bags plummeted down, falling on the exact spot where the girls had just been standing. "Thank you, Pam," Charlene gasped, "you saved my life!" "I didn't do anything," Pam stammered. "I thought you pushed me!" No human hand had touched either of them.

A grateful family thanked God in worship that night. No one doubted that angels had intervened to protect them that day. God had fulfilled for them His promise: "For He shall give His angels charge over you, to keep you in all your ways. They shall bear you up in their hands, lest you dash your foot against a stone" (Ps. 91:11, 12, N.K.J.V.).

Has your family ever sensed that the angels placed a protecting hedge around you? Ours has. My wife, Millie, our son Wes, and I were driving home to Michigan from Wes's graduation at Mount Pisgah Academy, North Carolina. As the sun lowered in the west, we interrupted our conversation and sang:

"I trust in God wherever I may be,
Upon the land or on the rolling sea.
Though come what may from day to day,
My heavenly Father watches over me."

We repeated a psalm and prayed, still speeding down the interstate highway. Three hours later, we threaded our way through a construction zone. At each bridge, arrows directed us to the left lane and a barrier walled off the right lane. Anxious to get home, I was driving too fast. We approached a bridge, and again a faint arrow painted on the pavement directed us to the left. I swung our Honda over to the left railing. As we came off the bridge we discovered, to our dismay, that the bridge dropped off twelve inches and our lane disappeared. Our light car bounced as we hit the hole. As I tried to steer back onto the main lane, the front wheel caught on the six-inch-high lip of the pavement. Now out of control, the car swerved across the lane close to the barrier on the right and then swung off the road on the left, veering sideways. It seemed we would roll over. We described an arc on the median. Millie screamed as she saw us cross the lanes of opposing traffic and head for the other barrier. And then, it appeared that we might careen down a thirty-foot embankment. But the car slid sharply left and came to a stop, facing the opposite direction we had been traveling. Our hearts were pounding. After gathering courage to examine the situation, we found that the only damage was one flat tire—its air seal broken by the sideways movement. In the few minutes it took us to change the tire, three more cars hit the same chuckhole, also almost going out of control.

Safely back on the road, we paused to thank God that we weren't killed or injured, that the car was unharmed, and that no other cars had been in the path of our vehicle after we crossed the median. As we were driving along meditating on God's protecting power, Wes thoughtfully remarked, "I'm so glad we had prayed for protection in worship tonight."

Spiritual Protection

However, the greatest danger that surrounds us is not physical danger or material loss. It is the evil powers that imperil our spiritual survival as Satan intrudes into homes unprotected by God's holy angels.

For example, the day began like any other for a Seventh-day Adventist family. During worship Dad asked God's protection over each family member, and, in their private devotions, he and his wife prayed for their 11-year-old son, Carl. Later that day, Carl came in from outdoors and asked, "Mom, may I ride my bike to town?"

"Why do you want to go?" Mom queried.

"Oh, I just want to," he answered.

"Well, what do you want to get?"

"Nothing special. I won't be long."

The more he insisted, the more her intuition convinced her that he should not go. "I sense that you have an urgency to go to town. Do you want to tell me why you want to go?"

Then with honesty he admitted that the neighbor boy had taught him to play cards, and that he now wanted to buy his own deck. Mother had had no idea that card playing might be a temptation to her son. She explained to him the dangers that card playing could lead to and suggested some other activity. The incident kept inexperienced feet from a dangerous path that could have led to gambling or other vices. The parents believe that heavenly agencies intervened in their son's case.

But family worship is not a magic wand, nor is Christianity a guarantee of protection insurance, else "believers" would fill the church's ranks. Sometimes our all-wise heavenly Father permits serious accidents to befall His trusting children. Our reason for celebrating family worship is not primarily to save ourselves from hardship or inconvenience. True, we covet God's protection that we may live to praise Him. But at the family altar we recognize our dependence on Him and we prize the opportunity to thank Him for sending His Son to die for us. Morning and evening we enjoy the fellowship of communing with the rest of the family—both heavenly and earthly.

"Come in humility with a heart full of tenderness and with a sense of the temptations and dangers before yourselves and your children; by faith bind them upon the altar, entreating for them the care of the Lord. Ministering angels will guard children who are thus dedicated to God. It is the duty of Christian parents, morning and evening, by earnest prayer and persevering faith, to make a hedge about their children."—*Testimonies*, vol. 1, pp. 397, 398.

By worshiping, we cultivate family togetherness and minister to one another's needs. At the family altar we join our hearts into one and witness to an onlooking universe that Jesus is Lord of our lives, and that we are on His side in the struggle against the enemy of our children and ourselves.

For Your Family

Following are six different worship activities from which you could choose opportune ideas for your family altar:

1. Read angel stories in *The Story of Redemption.* Make a list of what the angels did on different occasions such as:
   a. The crossing of the Red Sea (p. 124).
   b. Jesus' baptism (p. 196).
   c. Christ's crucifixion (pp. 213, 214).
   d. Peter's imprisonment (pp. 293-295).
   e. Discuss how angels might be intervening in our lives.
2. Read about the first Battle of Manassas (also called the Battle of Bull Run, Virginia) when an angel intervened in this great encounter of the Civil War. (See *Testimonies,* vol. 1, pp. 266, 267.)
   a. Ask family members: Can you think of any other battles where an angel might have intervened? Possible answers: George Washington's successful retreat from Long Island under cover of fog when the British had him trapped; Sennacherib's defeat (2 Kings 19:35); et cetera.
   b. Have you ever had any personal battles, perhaps with Satan, where you felt that an angel intervened to help you win?

3. This is a more complete outline for an evening worship. Topic—"Our Guardian Angel." Song. Prayer—"May we feel Your presence as we worship You. Send Your angels to join us here." Bible reading—Ps. 34:7. Ellen White reading—*Early Writings,* p. 39. Thought questions for the family:
   a. What have angels done for me/us?
   b. Where are our angels now?
   c. When have angels kept me from yielding to temptation?
   d. Does your guardian angel have a name? What name would you like to give your angel?

   Prayer.
4. Topic—"The Angels at Jesus' Birth." Song—"Hark, the Herald Angels Sing." Bible reading—Luke 2:1-21. What part did angels play in the story of Christ's birth? Ellen White reading—*The Great Controversy,* pp. 313-315.
   a. What did the searching angel almost do?
   b. Would the angel have found our family looking for Jesus' first coming if we had lived then? What about His second coming?

   Prayer—"Open our eyes to the events that tell us You are returning. May Your angel find us watching."
5. Topic—"Evil Angels." Prayer—"May Jesus' presence through the Holy Spirit visit our worship. Remove any evil angels that would bring disharmony." Activity—Have the participants see how many activities of the evil angels they can find in the passages read. Ellen White reading—*The Story of Redemption,* pp. 202, 203; *Testimonies,* vol. 1, p. 302; *Early Writings,* pp. 191, 192.
6. Topic—"Satan and the Evil Angels at the Death of Christ." Bible reading—Matt. 27:45-50; Mark

15:33-39; Luke 23:32-34; John 19:23-30. Ellen White reading—*The Story of Redemption*, pp. 230-232, 240.

a. What did the evil angels do when the good angel came down from heaven to open Christ's tomb?

b. What does the victory of Christ on the cross mean to our family?

c. Do you want to be on Satan's side or on Jesus' side?

d. Do we acknowledge that Satan is a defeated foe and that we have power through Christ to live a victorious Christian life? [Prepare a little scroll with these words on it: "I acknowledge that Satan is a defeated foe. I claim through the blood of Jesus the power to live a victorious Christian life." Invite the members of the family to sign the scroll.]

Note: For further study on angels use the Bible concordance and *The Comprehensive Index to the Writings of Ellen G. White.*

Family Worship From Eden to Eden

Family worship is a golden chain that connects Eden to Eden. Let's examine some of the links between the original home of the first family and Paradise restored.

Family Worship in the Garden of Eden

After a delightful day of smelling the fragrances of the blossoms, eating the luscious fruit, and training the vines into arbors for their new home, Adam and Eve watch the sun sink in the west. Heaven and earth seem ready to touch as the colors of gold, orange, pink, and purple flow across the sky. And then, wonder of wonders, the first pair hear the voice of God calling to them in the garden in the cool of the day. They answer their Creator Friend, invite Him into their new home, and with joy show Him the arbors of roses, bougainvillea, and orchids their hands have been weaving into living walls and roof. They raise their voices and sing praises to God, and God talks to them. The birds in their green cathedral pick up the strains and the angel choir all around them answers with a ten-part refrain. Adam's and Eve's hearts burn within them as their unimpaired six or seven—or possibly ten—senses register in their unforgetting memories, the beauty of it all. Jesus assures them of His unfailing love, and as He returns heavenward, He says, "Lo, I am with you alway." They stop and just listen. A gentle lion nearby purrs. The animals, each in his own language, praise their Maker as they prepare for the night's repose. A perfect day has ended.

(That was *worship*—what has to happen when

Creator and creature meet together in understanding relationship. And just think, God had planned that an eternity of even happier days should follow for Adam and Eve, their children, their great-great-great-grandchildren—and down to us—as we learned to know God.)

The cooing of the mourning doves awakens them the following morning when the sun peeps over the rolling hills. Their first thoughts are of praise to God. In rapturous joy they sing glory to their Friend. Overflowing love for beauty beyond imagination fills their hearts with praise to their Creator. A passing cheetah pauses to listen as heaven and earth blend their voices in praise. Other worlds look on with delight. A harmonious melody sweetens the atmosphere of their perfect garden slightly damp with the morning dew.

Nature, with the fragrance of its delicate flowers, blends its note of joy into the incense of praise and worship. The perfect landscape foliage speaks of God's great love and law. What heights of ecstasy when Adam and Eve "converse with leaf and flower and tree, gathering from each the secrets of its life" (*Patriarchs and Prophets*, p. 51)!

Can you add to this already majestic scene by imagining God Himself being there, quietly instructing and sharing in their excitement of discovering the marvels of the universe? During those early hours of worship, Adam and Eve learned the mysteries of Creation from the lips of the Creator. Each discovery must have deepened their respect for the Father. Greater love and gratitude overflowed into praise and worship. Daily they became more in tune with the divine music of love that filled an unfallen world.

Abraham—The Altar Builder

"Look at yonder sojourner. This evening I see him again gather his household, even as he did this morning.

I've noticed his altars in other parts of the land. He builds them wherever he goes. And he sets them up in the open, never in a grove. Look at how carefully he arranges the wood. He is going to slay that lamb!"

The other observer answers, "Let's go a little closer. What does this mean?" The two curious men edge toward the encampment. They watch the fire consuming the body of the slain lamb and hear the venerable patriarch speaking to his God as the family joins him, kneeling in a circle around the altar.

"We choose You, Lord. Our only hope is in the merits of the blood which You will pour out someday to save us. Thank You, Lord, for covering the sins of our family—of Sarah, of Isaac, of Ishmael—all of us. Make us safe in the blood." The children who love the lamb and hate to see it die shed tears over it. They sing a song of praise, embrace one another, and return to their evening chores as the smoke from the altar seems to waft their prayers heavenward.

"I think," the first observer breaks the silence, "I think that this God is different from those of Canaan. He talks to his God as he would with a friend. Could this be the secret of the kindness of this man? Could it be that from that altar comes the power that makes this family so different from the people of Canaan?"

The Bible describes Abraham as an altar builder. Notice what it says happened at the altar. "There builded he an altar *unto the Lord, who appeared unto him*" (Gen. 12:7). When he moved to Bethel—where years later his grandson Jacob would see the dream of the heavenly ladder—the Bible says, "There he builded an altar unto the Lord, and *called upon the name of the Lord*" (verse 8).

After Abraham had lied and misrepresented God in Egypt, and become disappointed at his own lack of faith, he went back to Bethel, where God had appeared to him before. Penitent hands rebuilt the old altar, "and there

Abram called on the name of the Lord" (Gen. 13:4).

We receive the legacy of the family altar from the patriarchs of old. The first altar specifically mentioned in the Bible is that of Noah in Genesis 8:20. God had remembered him and his family during the terrible storm, and Noah's first act upon leaving the ark was to gather his family together and to remember God. In gratitude he reared an altar and sacrificed.

The first children born into our world built altars. The Bible tells of the sacrifices of Cain and Abel, and we can assume that they made them on altars.

Other Family Altars

Fires of other family altars, about which we know little, have changed the course of history. Wouldn't it be wonderful to peep into those hidden years at Nazareth and to eavesdrop as Joseph read from the scrolls of the prophets or the psalms? Busy, trying to eke out a living for his family, he finds time before opening up his carpenter's shop and after closing its doors, to gather Mary and the children around the family altar. His wife notes the ready responses of the child Jesus and treasures them in her heart as she sees her firstborn increasing "in wisdom and stature, and in favour with God and man" (Luke 2:52). Holy lamps of sacrifice are kindled there, and resolves are crystallizing that ultimately will bring eternal salvation within your reach and mine.

Family Worship in a "Divided Home"

Timothy must have been a lad of about 15 when Paul met him at Lystra around A.D. 45. The fickle mob had dragged Paul out of the city and stoned him. Probably Timothy joined the group that surrounded Paul's apparently lifeless body. With joy they received the battered and crushed man of God when he stirred and then arose. Some Bible scholars believe that Paul stayed that night in Timothy's home, recuperating from the attack on his life. If so, he likely observed the religious practices of Eunice, Timothy's mother, and Lois, his grandmother, who were Christian believers. The lad's father was a Greek (Acts 16:1).

Some mothers in a divided-home situation feel that they can do little to transmit a religious heritage. Not so with Eunice. Paul writes to Timothy, "From a child thou hast known the holy scriptures, which are able to make thee wise unto salvation through faith which is in Jesus Christ" (2 Tim. 3:15). Elsewhere he said, "I call to remembrance the unfeigned faith that is in thee, which dwelt first in thy grandmother Lois, and thy mother Eunice; and I am persuaded that in thee also" (chap. 1:5).

Timothy's mother and grandmother set the pattern, establishing his faith in the Holy Scriptures. When we do not take the time to gather our children for worship, or to model Christ's tenderness, what are we robbing them of? Their chance to absorb and develop love and faith as Timothy did under Lois and Eunice. And you, grandmothers, never underestimate the importance of your continuing prayers for your children and grandchildren.

"Religion was the atmosphere of his [Timothy's] home. The piety of his homelife was not of a cheap order, but pure, sensible, and uncorrupted by false sentiments. Its moral influence was substantial, not fitful, not impulsive, not changeable."—Ellen G. White, in *The Youth's Instructor,* May 5, 1898.

"Unfeigned faith" means a steady and persistent faith. Although Timothy had no outstanding talents *(ibid.),* his early home training made him a dependable missionary whom Paul could send on the most delicate and confidential missions. His last book he wrote to Timothy upon whom the aged apostle laid his mantle.

What good did Eunice do in emphasizing the family

altar with her son, Timothy? Only eternity will reveal the influence of that heritage of faith in its ever-broadening lines, transmitted by this almost-unknown mother by the fireside in that "divided home" in Lystra.

Family Worship in the New Earth

Our family has had worship in some strange places over the years. We have prayed atop Mount Elbert, Colorado's highest peak, and been spared in a turbulent thunderstorm that left us unscathed, although Millie felt the electrical charge as lightning hit right next to us. In the Dominican Republic we have worshiped beneath the coconut palms with the ocean waves splashing on the beach. While riding in jet planes in awe, we watched the sun, like a flaming red ball, sink into the waters of the ocean. We have worshiped in our mountain cabin when a spring snowstorm—breathtaking in its beauty—surprised our family get-together. And we have celebrated our family altar on the rim of the Grand Canyon. But all these memories will be nothing compared to family worship in the new earth.

"Wes, you choose where we'll have worship this evening."

"Great, let's fly through the rings of Saturn, buzz that canyon fifty miles deep on the planet Zeno in the constellation of Sagittarius, and then catch up to Mr. and Mrs. Enoch, who are visiting the planet Lapo 25 billion light-years away!"

We travel at the speed of thought. "Let's invite Grandpa and Grandma to join us," John suggests. No more arthritis or heart disease! Our tireless flight carries us to worlds afar. Wes does a cartwheel over Majestic Canyon while John "scuba dives" in Bottomless Lake fifty miles below. Now on to Lapo.

"Hello, Enoch, it's good to see you again!" He turns and says, "Yes, here are our friends from Planet Earth!"

And as the family gathers around, the patriarch says, "Tell the Mrs. and me what it was like to live on earth in the days when all your generation made its decision for or against Christ. How did it seem to you to be redeemed out of the wicked world?"

John and Wes, Grandpa and Grandma, and all the family tell the experience. Millie enthusiastically starts to describe the great final movements that in a few short weeks proclaimed around the world the gospel story of a crucified and soon-coming Jesus, and the rest of the family add personal details. Bonnie, my first wife, whose frame had wasted away with cancer while on earth, is now with us, blessed with a new glorious body and eternal youth. (Don't worry, there won't be any competition. God will take care of all that, too.)

Nearby, angels look on in amazement, but "as we tell redemption's story, they will fold their wings, for angels never knew the joy which our salvation brings." We speak of the cataclysmic events of the end of the world, but the new heaven and new earth are so wonderful that our greatest trials seem to be fading from our memories. "Hallelujah!" our voices ring out in rapturous song. "Heaven is cheap enough. It was worth it all. Glory be to the Father and unto the Lamb and to the Holy Spirit forever and ever. Thank You, Jesus, for so great a salvation. Hallelujah! Praise the Lord!"

Basics of a Family Altar

We've taken a panoramic view of the family altar from Eden to Eden. What do the basics of family worship seem to be, deduced from the Biblical records?

The purpose of the "family altar" is first and foremost *to adore our Lord*. It is next *to renew the family covenant* with God and one another. The altar is a place *to sacrifice*—where we claim the blood of the Lamb of God for forgiveness, protection, and victory. It is a place *to instruct* so that in an atmosphere of warmth and acceptance we can transmit our religious heritage and family values from generation to generation (Deut. 6:6-9). Last, the altar is also a place *to celebrate familyness.* In Bible times God's people erected altars to celebrate or to commemorate events (Joshua 22:26-28, 34).

Family altars need continual care. In Biblical times God gave specific instructions that His people should use no mortar in rearing an altar. If not cared for, the stones of the altar would tumble down and get trodden under foot of men or animals. As they lovingly replaced the stones, the patriarchs were, no doubt, reminded of the importance they placed upon the altar's function. No, the family altar cannot be built once and for all, then or now. Faithful guarding of a family altar today against the many distractions from it requires careful attention.

The patriarchs never built their altars in woods or near trees. Immoral practices carried on in groves characterized the pagan shrines. Today our family altars should be different from worldly customs or practices. TV has become the modern altar of Baal in many homes. God always asks for undivided loyalty, and will not share a worship spot with any other god.

The priest of the family laid the sacrifice on the altar morning and evening. We do well to have a specific time for family worship, and to celebrate it regularly because we should face the issues of today by today's dedication and prayer, not yesterday's.

The father led the family devotions as the priest of the household. His duty, established by God, continued throughout his life. In cases of an absent father or an unbelieving one, the mother took charge of family worship.

The gathering around the altar is a corporate act of family witness that demonstrates that it chooses God and His way. It is an occasion for meeting God, for entering into relationship and friendship with Him.

The focal point of the family altar is the blood—the merits of the blood of Jesus to save us from sin. By faith—claiming the power of that blood—we place a protective mark or seal on the family so that the destroyer cannot harm us.

Worship Definition

What is worship?

Worship is the wonder of the creature as he senses the presence of his Creator. It is showing respect and reverence for God by one who feels unworthy. Through it we know God, become acquainted with Him as a friend, and adore Him for His many gifts, including the forgiveness of sin. We enter into covenant relationship with Him. When this happens in a family setting, it designates the family as the property of God, as sealed and safe in the blood of Jesus, thus drawing the members close to God and to one another. This is family worship.

For Your Family

Suggested Worship Activities

With these activities include an appropriate song known by the family, a short opening prayer inviting God's presence, and a closing prayer. We have planned these worships to be active and not passive. You can assign different members of the family to prepare and lead in the worship responsibilities.

1. Topic—"The First Sunset Worship in Eden." Bible reading—Gen. 1 and Gen. 2:1-3. Ellen G. White reading—*Patriarchs and Prophets*, pp. 46, 47.

a. Imagine what the first Friday evening was like when Adam and Eve celebrated the beginning of the first Sabbath on earth. Be creative in thought.

b. Ask the Lord to help you to have beautiful Friday evening worships in remembrance of that Creation week.

2. Topic—"Worship in Heaven." Bible reading—Rev. 22:3. Ellen G. White reading—*Patriarchs and Prophets,* p. 357.

   a. Discuss what worship is like in heaven now and what it will be like when we get there.

   b. As a family, how can we make our worship of the King of kings and Lord of lords more meaningful and beautiful? List the various ideas of the group.

   ____

   ____

   Prayer—"Teach us how to worship You in the manner of which You are worthy."

3. Topic—"Jesus as a Child." Bible reading—Luke 2:52. Ellen G. White reading—*The Desire of Ages,* pp. 69, 70.

   a. Jesus learned from His parents and from God as we do. Discuss how your family can discover more of God's truth and will.

   b. What spiritual areas do the family members feel they want to learn more about? List four or five examples.

   ____

   ____

   c. Assign different family members to work on these topics to present at family worship.

4. **A Memory Text for fathers** and family members that all can repeat often at the beginning or at the end of worship—

" 'But I and my family, we will worship the Lord' " (Joshua 24:15, N.E.B.).
A younger member of the family can make a colorful plaque or scroll quoting this text and inserting the family name.

5. **A Suggested FAMILY COVENANT** (you could make it into a scroll and frame and place it on the wall of the usual worship room):

"We the __________ family enter into a covenant with each other to seek the Lord with all our hearts and souls. It is our desire to determine to have family worship morning and evening as a priority in our home. We desire Christ through the Holy Spirit to be our teacher."

(Signed) ______________
____
____
____

(Date) ______________

Elijah Speaks to Families

" 'Elijah truly is coming first and will restore all things' " (Matt. 17:11, N.K.J.V.).

Drought and famine grip the land nearly nine centuries before Christ. Almost all the cattle are dead. Thousands of children are dying from malnutrition and starvation. King Ahab and his royal court ascend the sun-parched slope of Mount Carmel. Four hundred and fifty prophets of Baal take their place around the altar of their god. Close behind them stand four hundred prophets of Asherah, surrounding the sacred wood statue of their goddess of fertility, beneath the now leafless trees of their grove.

Opposite this imposing retinue stands one lone man—his dress simple, his features rugged. His name *Elijah,* given him by unknown parents of the eastern province of Gilead, means "Jehovah is my God." He stands beside a broken-down altar of twelve stones where years ago families used to worship, before the Baal altars had become so popular.

Elijah speaks, and his voice echoes to the tens of thousands of Israel who have gathered on the ridges and in the valley below. " 'How long will you go limping with two different opinions? If the Lord is God, follow Him; but if Baal, then follow him' " (1 Kings 18:21, R.S.V.). The word *Baal* means "lord." The religion of Baal—corrupted by immorality, by drunkenness, by gross idolatry—negated everything that Jehovah commanded.

The pagan priests build an altar for Baal, and an impressive and sophisticated ceremony takes place.

They speak beautiful words, and ecstatic rites follow. No one could question that Baal's devotees believe in their god. In fact they are willing to shed their own blood right there to prove it. But, there is no fire—no power!

Isn't that the way it is when one worships other gods—even the popular ones of the twentieth century? Man is a worshiping creature. He is always worshiping someone or something. If it's not the true God, he will find a substitute—maybe even himself.

After about six hours of calling on Baal, jumping on the altar, and cutting themselves with knives, silence descends upon the mountain. The prophets of Baal are hoarse, bleeding, exhausted. There is still no fire, no sign that any god hears. They retire from the contest.

At the hour of the evening sacrifice, Elijah steps forward. Surveying much of the nation of Israel, his eyes seem to pierce their souls. In their faces he reads the tragic stories of those who have sought for happiness at other altars, who have worshiped money, lust, prestige, pleasure. He sees the childless arms of mothers who have sacrificed the lives of their children for the "good life" in their culture. The broken marriages and the broken hearts which fill the country meet his gaze.

His great heart yearns in love for the deluded people. In invitation he stretches out his arms and asks them to approach him. "And all the people came near unto him. And he repaired the altar of the Lord that was broken down" (verse 30). The way back to God begins with the repairing of the abandoned altar. Elijah doesn't build an altar just any way he wants to—he constructs it according to the instructions that God Himself had given hundreds of years before. And he erects the "altar in the name of the Lord" (verse 32). The moral depravity of the people, the rampant disregard of others, the commandment breaking is because the people have not sought God as their first priority, have not sought a friendship with Him. Right where the ruin began, Elijah starts the return.

Is it not time now to heed the Elijah message and rebuild the family altar for heart-tuning within the home?

Rebuilding the Family Altar Among Seventh-day Adventists Today

To an alarming extent Seventh-day Adventists are coming to resemble the world that surrounds them. The lives of thousands testify that their unspoken creed is "We will be as the heathen, as the families of the countries" (Eze. 20:32).

The only way out is worship—*intelligent worship.* The apostle Paul gives us the clarion call:

"With eyes wide open to the mercies of God, I beg you, my brothers, as an act of intelligent worship, to give him your bodies, as a living sacrifice, consecrated to him and acceptable by him. Don't let the world around you squeeze you into its own mould, but let God re-make you so that your whole attitude of mind is changed. Thus you will prove in practice that the will of God's good, acceptable to him and perfect" (Rom. 12:1, 2, Phillips).

How many Seventh-day Adventist homes are worshiping God intelligently with a regular family altar, remolding their minds and practices from within? A survey published in the *Adventist Review,* April 21, 1983, found that from the 8,223 Seventh-day Adventist homes surveyed, 28 percent "always" had daily worship and another 20.3 percent "usually" had family worship. The family worshipers reported a significant difference from the non-family worshipers in personal study of the Bible and the writings of Ellen White, in assurance of being right with God, in successful witnessing, and in a positive attitude toward their local church. No one knows how many Seventh-day Adventist homes have both regular morning *and* evening worship. We can only conjecture that the percentages conducting twice-a-day worship would be considerably less and the potential benefits considerably more.

The next question we need to ask is How many families find spiritual strength and fellowship with God and one another in the worship experience? We fear that some families who have regular family worship find it little more than a form and that in some cases the children and parents are not discovering in it a true source of power to successfully meet the multiple problems which accost family harmony and purpose.

Do Seventh-day Adventist Christians think family worship is important? Yes, definitely! But they have problems. We have taken the pulse of their concerns in marriage and family seminars in various countries. A group of young couples married four to six months listed "family worship" as their top priority problem. Couples request help: "We're not having worship, but we know we should. How do we get started?" Ministers and their wives say, "We want to have worship twice daily, but frankly, we're too busy to have family worship." Some wives report, "My husband can pray with everyone but me." Mothers say, "I have to conduct the worship at home because my husband won't accept the priesthood of the family." Fathers complain, "I've run out of ideas; what's new?"

Most of us realize that Christ has to be the center of our homes. We've heard for years that a home is like a wheel with Christ at the hub, and the family members as the spokes. The closer we get to Christ the hub, the closer we come together. We believe this. The trouble lies in implementing it. We realize in some vague way that in order to make Christ the center of our homes, we need to have family worship. But when we attempt to do this, worship often turns out to be a drag rather than a delight, and we get discouraged. Consequently, many homes have given up trying to have family worship at all. It just doesn't seem to work.

One of the greatest things that we could do for the home today—even the Adventist home—is the rebuilding and revitalization of the family altar. Ellen G. White observes: "If ever there was a time when every house should be a house of prayer, it is now. Infidelity and skepticism prevail. Iniquity abounds. . . . And yet, in this time of fearful peril, some who profess to be Christians have no family worship. They do not honor God in the home, they do not teach their children to love and fear Him."—*Child Guidance,* p. 517. Again, she tells us: "Fathers and mothers should often lift up their hearts to God in humble supplication for themselves and their children. Let the father, as priest of the household, lay upon the altar of God the morning and evening sacrifice, while the wife and children unite in prayer and praise. In such a household Jesus will love to tarry."—*Patriarchs and Prophets,* p. 144.

Ellen White did not consider family prayer to be an optional thing—good, if you have time for it. Listen to how strongly she felt about this: "I know of nothing that causes me so great sadness as a prayerless home. I do not feel safe in such a house for a single night; and were it not for the hope of helping the parents to realize their necessity and their sad neglect, I would not remain."—*Signs of the Times,* Aug. 7, 1884.

What Will Happen When Altars Are Rebuilt?

The scene that follows the rebuilding of the altar on Mount Carmel is one of the most dramatic in Bible history. Elijah offers a prayer. Not flowery or complicated, it is only about thirty seconds long. See the prophet kneeling beside the altar, hands outstretched. He pleads the merits of the blood to cover the sins of the people. "And it came to pass at the time of the offering of the evening sacrifice, that Elijah the prophet came near, and said, Lord God of Abraham, Isaac, and of Israel, let it be known this day that thou art God in Israel. . . . Hear me, O Lord, hear me, that this people may know that thou art the Lord God, and that thou hast *turned their heart* back again" (1 Kings 18:36, 37).

"Then the fire of the Lord fell." The marvel of the story is that the fire, instead of falling on the sinful people, fell upon the innocent victim. The shed blood of Jesus claimed at that altar covered the sinners and permitted the penitent to respond: "The Lord, he is the God; the Lord, he is the God."

Today the TV altar has displaced the family altar in millions of homes. Parents wonder why they find no fire, no power in their spiritual lives, why temptation so easily overcomes their children. Parents must sense the dangers that their children face. We need to claim the victory for our families available to us in the blood of Christ. Ministering angels will guard our children when we have thus dedicated them to God.

The consecrating fire of God will fall upon dedicated children, and the showers of the latter rain upon worshiping families. Then all will know that Jehovah is God, and that there is none else. And remember—it all begins with a father and mother who repair "the altar of the Lord that was broken down."

As the family on earth gathers around their altar, they enter by faith into the Holy of Holies in heaven while they claim the merits of their great High Priest and pour out their praise and petition before the throne of grace. God is *measuring* our personal and family devotions. "Then I was given a reed like a measuring rod. And the angel stood, saying, 'Rise and measure the temple of God, the altar, and those who worship there' " (Rev. 11:1, N.K.J.V.).

The hour of God's judgment has come (see Rev. 14:7). As Jesus ministers the benefits of His atonement we need to be in daily touch with the cosmic issues about us. As the Messenger of the covenant ministers for us, the other messenger (the first one mentioned in Malachi 3:1) must do his work on earth—"and he shall *prepare the way* before me." Isaiah said: "The voice of him that crieth in the wilderness, Prepare ye the way of the Lord, make straight in the desert a highway for our God. . . . The crooked shall be made straight, and the rough places plain: and the glory of the Lord shall be revealed" (chap. 40:3-5).

Elijah himself was not to appear. John the Baptist disclaimed being the reincarnation of that prophet. But he did a mighty work " in the spirit and power of Elijah" (Luke 1:17, R.S.V.), restoring all things, and preparing the way for the first coming of Christ.

Now, at the end of the age, "before the coming of the great and dreadful day of the Lord," a mighty work must take place. Elijah himself will not reappear (those who expect him will be as disappointed as were the literalist Jews who rejected John), but a prophetic message goes forth proclaimed "in the spirit and power of Elijah." Its purpose will be to restore *all things*—every institution marred by sin—back to their pristine beauty. All will be reset in the lives of God's chosen as a witness to His glory—marriage, the family, the Sabbath. Each will occupy the place and fulfill the function that God intended.

"And they that shall be of thee shall build the old waste places: thou shalt raise up the foundations of many generations; and thou shalt be called, The repairer of the breach, The restorer of paths to dwell in" (Isa. 58:12).

God's people will restore the breach in both the Sabbath and the family commandments. They will reset the two beautiful gifts entrusted to man in Eden like God's jewels in His jewel case.

Sin, which is basically the breaking of relationships, will be put away under this mighty message, marriage oneness will be restored, alienated children and parents will draw together, and broken hearts will be healed.

"Behold, I will send you Elijah the prophet before the coming of the great and dreadful day of the Lord: And he shall *turn the heart of the fathers to the children, and the heart of the children to their fathers,* lest I come and smite the earth with a curse" (Mal. 4:5, 6). When our hearts have been turned to God, they will be in tune with Him and all those around us.

For Your Family

Suggested Worship Activities

1. Topic—"Have We Ever Climbed Mount Carmel?" Bible reading—1 Kings 18:17-46. What message does the Lord have for our family in this story? Which of the following might be gods* in our home?

____ambition	____movies	____housework
____sports	____money	____work
____pleasure	____education	____entertainment
____rock music	____friends	____TV
____fashions	____popularity	____possessions

*A god is someone or something that keeps us from worshiping Jesus with the whole heart. Do we love some of the above more than we love God?

2. Topic—"Our Family Altar." Ellen G. White reading—*Prophets and Kings,* pp. 144-154 (may be read as a continuous story for three to four worships). How can we start to build or rebuild our family altar?

Decide	**Family Vote—YES**	**NO**
a. Will family worship be daily?	____	____
b. Will family worship be morning and evening?	____	____

c. What time in the morning?______ In the evening?______

d. How long will worship last?______

e. Who will be responsible for worship?

	Sun.	Mon.	Tue.	Wed.	Thurs	Fri.	Sab.
Morning	____	____	____	____	____	____	____
Evening	____	____	____	____	____	____	____

f. To start with, what worship materials do we wish to use?______________________________

____

3. Topic—"My Choice." Bible reading—1 Kings 18:37-39; Matt. 3:11.
   a. If Elijah told you, "Choose Baal or choose God!" which one would you choose?________
   b. Do we want power and fire within our family worship? Yes ____ No ____ Why? __________
   c. Which of these steps might help so that God can bless us fully?

____ Accept Jesus as Lord of our lives.
____ Love the Lord with all our hearts.
____ Keep God's commandments.

____ Repent of our sins and ask forgiveness.
____ Make things right with family members and others.
____ Love one another as a family.
____ Ask the Holy Spirit to bless the family and worship.
____ Invite Jesus and His angels to join our worship gathering.
____ Remove idols from our lives.

d. What steps must we take to start doing the above?

____

____

e. Just for interest and evaluation, how many hours does each member spend watching TV?

Name	*Hours per Day*	*Hours per Week*
________	________	________
________	________	________
________	________	________
________	________	________

Are you satisfied with the amount?
If not, what can each person do to change?

Where Have the Fathers Gone?

"And, ye fathers, provoke not your children to wrath: but bring them up in the nurture and admonition of the Lord" (Eph. 6:4).

Suitcases, sleeping bags, food, skateboards, and three teenagers filled every inch of our little Honda wagon speeding south—Florida-bound! Sixteen hours later skateboard wheels screeched in the Florida sunshine. Up the twelve-foot sides of the empty swimming pool in the skateboarding park the boys went—with only one wheel on the tiles and three in the air. Then zoom—back into a power dive. Our son Wes and his two friends had planned the trip and shared the gas expense. At that time Michigan had no skateboarding parks and one thing that Wes wanted to do was to go skateboarding at a real park. The closest facilities were hundreds of miles away.

The three skated six hours on Friday, more on Saturday night, and continued the pace on Sunday until 4:00 P.M. Then we piled back into the Honda and arrived home totally exhausted for work and school Monday morning. It was not exactly my idea of a restful weekend, but worth it for the relationship it afforded with my teenage son and his friends—doing something that Wes wanted to do.

How much time do we Christian fathers spend alone with our children? One group of boys, who checked with stopwatches, found that they had averaged seven and one-half minutes alone with their fathers during an entire week. When fathers do talk to their children it often involves giving them a command: "Take out the garbage"; "Wash your hands"; et cetera.

Where have the fathers gone? Many places. But of most concern is that they have gone out of the everyday lives of their children. Not only do many fathers have no relationship with them, but they also give little religious or moral education to their families.

A father and his young son walked together through the woods. In places the terrain was open and the little fellow ran ahead or found his own way around obstacles. But after a while they came to considerable undergrowth of brush and blackberry bushes. The boy missed the path and soon found himself entangled. "Daddy, my legs are getting scratched!" The father lifted him out of the briers and said, "Son, follow me and step where I step." Within a few minutes they had crossed the thorny place and arrived at their destination.

In life's journey, happy is the child who when his "legs are getting scratched" can find guidance and support from a wise and loving father. Such a parent doesn't just tell the child in family worship what to do, but *models* in his own Christian lifestyle the better way and can say, "Here, son, step where I step." A strong, warm father model in childhood can save children from many of the thorns of the way.

The Father's Role

Ellen White years ago gave us sound, considered guidance on how to prevent a myriad of problems that today we find associated with low father image. In 1905 she wrote: "The father should enforce in his family the sterner virtues—energy, integrity, honesty, patience, courage, diligence, and practical usefulness. And what he requires of his children he himself should practice, illustrating these virtues in his own manly bearing."—*The Ministry of Healing*, p. 391.

But assertiveness is not enough, for the statement goes on to say: "Combine affection with authority, kindness and sympathy with firm restraint. Give some of your leisure hours to your children; become acquainted with them; associate with them in their work and in their sports, and win their confidence. Cultivate friendship with them, especially with your sons. In this way you will be a strong influence for good."—*Ibid.*, pp. 391, 392.

Today, when his role is under fire and encroached upon from all sides, the father must stand up and be counted. He must not relinquish his God-given role or surrender it to the ideas of the debased contemporary culture. What does Christian fatherhood call for?

A father should be what he wants his family to be.

Will he shake the last drop out of the bottom of his cup, or will he give what is overflowing from his own full cup? Does dad come in "dry" to family worship and pick up some ready-mix or predigested pabulum? Does he bring in some stale bread, or does he have freshly baked shewbread warm from his personal fellowship with his Lord? He must have a warm, personal relationship with Jesus Christ that he can share. The father must seek from God before he is able to pass on the blessing to the family.

Like Abraham, commanding "his children and his household after him, and they shall keep the way of the Lord" (Gen. 18:19), the father should be the head of the house. God has ordained that he should be first. In what way? He should be the first to love; the first to say "I'm sorry"; the first to sacrifice—even life itself—for the well-being of his wife and children. Father should be the first to give and the first to share the bread of heaven with his family.

Matthew 20:25-28 explains two conflicting headship models. Christ said that the Gentiles exercise dominion *over* others, but that the Christian leader should follow the "servant model." In the servant relationship he is *among*, not *over*, those he leads. "And whosoever will be chief *among* you, let him be your servant: even as the Son of man came not to be ministered unto, but to minister, and to give his life a ransom for many."

Perhaps the best illustration of what Christian leadership is all about is the *shepherd model.* The true shepherd does not drive the sheep (authoritarian model). Nor does he lag behind the sheep and let them choose the way (laissez-faire model). Rather he goes before them, and the sheep, hearing his voice, know him and are known by him, and they follow him. Thus the Christian way is *authoritative* but not *authoritarian* leadership. The Christian father will lead by relationship, but always conscious of the divine authority vested in him to relate to his children and also to restrain them when necessary that they might know the way of the Lord. The Christian father-leader has "preferred outcomes," and, based on his knowledge of God's will, he leads the family toward those eternal goals.

An Initiator

To be an effective leader in the home, the father must take *initiative* in family values, goal setting, and decisions.

Years ago when our children were small, I read and tried to practice the teachings of several new books on group dynamics and decision-making. For several years I experimented with leaderless groups in the home setting. The idea was to create a leadership vacuum. Nature abhors a vacuum and will always try to fill it. When I didn't show structured leadership, then our children would rise to the occasion. From time to time I would intervene, but we had quite an emphasis on what I thought was "democratic leadership." Before long we the parents had relinquished control and found ourselves responding to the initiatives of our children. The boys were becoming rather "famous" in the neighborhood for being headstrong and self-willed. Through some difficult experiences it finally dawned on me that I must show the initiative and let *them* respond to me. Being peace-loving by nature, I found the transition rather difficult. I still believe in a "democratic family," but only if the father has preferred outcomes and is *authoritative* (not authoritarian)—taking the initiative in goal setting, especially where it concerns values.

Some have not grasped all the issues involved in family government. We think we are living the "Elijah message," but in reality it is the "Eli message." Eli loved peace and he indulged his sons. He reacted to their initiatives. "Now, boys, please don't do those things. These are not good reports that I hear. Be good boys!" But Hophni and Phinehas laughed under their breath. They knew that Dad wouldn't *do* anything. A few years told the story: thirty thousand men slain at Aphek, sons and father dead the same day, and the ark of God taken. Does the Eli message produce *heart-tuning?* No! Its indulgence brings *heart-breaking.*

The Biblical story of Dinah illustrates what happens when a father doesn't show initiative and decision. Jacob and family camped at Shechem. His daughter, Dinah, "went out to see the daughters of the land" (Gen. 34:1). You know the story. Prince Shechem seduced her and then came with his father, Hamor, to negotiate a marriage. Jacob vacillated. What should he do? He didn't know what to do—and so he did nothing. It created a leadership vacuum, which his sons filled. They took measures because their indecisive father failed to act. The affair resulted in a deceitful arrangement, followed by the slaughter of all the men of Shechem. What could Jacob have done? Step number 1: "Where is Dinah?" She had been left in the young man's house. Was it God's will? Action plan: "We don't even talk until Dinah is back under my roof!" By resolute decision Jacob could have controlled a difficult situation instead of letting it overwhelm him.

Yes, God has called the father to take initiative in family decision-making. He also expects him to act as a "house band" (that is what *husband* means) in binding the whole family together in warm relationship.

Father Deprivation and Child Adjustment

More than 10 percent—about 8 million—of the children in the United States live in fatherless homes at any given time. Three times that number are fatherless for a significant part of their childhood. In some areas of the large cities more than 50 percent of the children are fatherless. However, the most widespread problem is not father absence, dismal as that picture is. The greater threat is father neglect where fathers live with their families but have lost close, regular contact with their children.[1]

Psychiatrist Irving Bieber, of New York Medical College, conducted a nine-year study of homosexuals undergoing psychotherapy. He declares that he has never interviewed a homosexual who had a close and warm relationship with his father.[2] Psychologist Henry B. Biller says that studies of the family backgrounds of both male and female homosexuals uncover a high occurrence of father deprivation.[3]

Father presence or involvement tends to have a positive effect on a daughter's relationship with boys. Girls deprived of a father because of divorce are more

---

[1] Henry Biller and Dennis Meredith, *Father Power* (New York: David McKay Co., 1975), pp. 8, 9.

[2] *Ibid.*, p. 172.

[3] Lester Velie, "Where Have All the Fathers Gone?" *Reader's Digest*, April, 1973, p. 157.

likely to become "boy-crazy" as they mistakenly seek appreciation from a father figure, while those whose fathers have died may tend to avoid boys.[4]

A lack of father involvement with the child tends to decrease the child's analytical ability and his ability for productive thinking (translating great plans into appropriate action).[5]

Certainly we find some wonderful fatherless or father-neglected families that have successfully reared sons and daughters to form happy, well-adjusted homes of their own. However, the task seems to be so much easier and more delightful when the father is a strong, dynamic figure in the everyday life of the children.

Fun Fatherhood

"I didn't have time for my oldest son," the minister began his story, "and by the age of 12, he didn't have time for me. I had to a great degree lost him and my influence for good on his life. When his brother came along I stopped and took an inventory. My conclusion: I had deprived my son of knowing his father, but more than that, I had deprived myself of the privilege of fun fatherhood—of having a warm, meaningful relationship with my son. I made a new resolution right there. The oldest son still doesn't let me all the way into his circle, but I'm enjoying being a father as I never did before."

A seminary student told us that when his oldest son was 9, he realized he didn't know him. To avoid it happening with the three younger children, he decided to change his priorities and get to understand his son for the first time. He bought cross-country skis for the whole family, even his 3-year-old daughter. Sundays he put away the books, and together the troop of six headed out

[4] Biller and Meredith, *op. cit.*, pp. 176, 177.
[5] *Ibid.*, pp. 211-215.

across Michigan's snow-covered fields. Later he bought bicycles for the family. They decided "oneness was family togetherness."

Fathers who take initiative in developing "family-ness" enjoy a variety of relationship activities with their sons and daughters. One father who travels considerably takes his sons with him on his business trips. A truck driver has as his traveling companion a different child each week during summer vacation time. The children began to see the world and the world of their father as well.

In one home a visitor might have heard the father singing, "Don't sit under the apple tree with anyone else but me," as he and the 4-year-old daughter crouched under the make-believe apple tree (the grand piano). Hide-and-seek, a bumpy camel ride on her dad's back, special stories with all kinds of strange sound effects, were part of this daughter's exciting childhood. Her father was a very important person in her life. She knows without a doubt that she is considered special and is loved. Now that 4-year-old is a lovely Christian teenager with high Christian standards.

One father and teenage daughter have a special relationship in the physical-fitness program. Not only do they play tennis together but football as well. Sunday afternoon is their special time. Sometimes they watch a ball game on TV. During halftime they rush outside to kick the ball and throw a few passes. In the evening the father, mother, and daughter talk naturally about spiritual concerns and at times join in a lively discussion on politics.

A ride to the junk yard looking for parts to use on the old jalopy is an important event for another son. Soon one observes four legs protruding from under the old car as they work together on "their" project of making their pride and joy run. When it's time to do some missionary endeavor there's no hassle. It's just another fun time when the family shares with others.

Jesus, in Mark 9:12, spoke of the Elijah prophecy referring to John the Baptist and said that this work *"restoreth all things."* It must restore fathers to an active, involved, even powerful, position in the lives of their children. How else can one fulfill Malachi 4:6? "And he shall turn the heart of the fathers to the children, and the heart of the children to their fathers." It is never too late to begin.

Hints for Father-Children Activities

1. Take your children on a camping trip, leaving most of the organization and work to the youngsters.
2. Play table games with the whole family.
3. Join in games and sports with the children and their friends.
4. Take children on Sabbath walks out in nature.
5. Have separate worships with each child once a week.
6. Work with children on a "My Life Notebook."
7. Tell child once or twice a week that you will spend a certain amount of time with him on a project of his choice, such as working on his bike or helping with multiplication tables.
8. Work on Adventist Youth Honors with the children.
9. When traveling, write a specific letter or card to each child or phone him or her at an appointed time.
10. For children away at school, cut out clippings from local papers about friends, activities, and events, and send them with a newsy home letter.
11. Take boys shopping, looking for men's things.
12. Work together with boys on household repairs.
13. Take a child to your place of business and if possible have him help with some small duty for a short

period of time.

14. Read to the children on a certain night of the week.

15. Listen to their stories and help them solve their problems.

16. Take classes together with children.

17. Take each child separately on a dinner date.

18. Help the child to plan surprises of special kindness for mother and different children.

19. Give the child a variety of enriching experiences and then encourage him according to his natural bent.

20. Teach the father's trade or hobby to the children.

21. Join small children in their pretend world.

22. Enter into feelings of the child, accepting them even though they may differ from yours.

23. Tell each child he or she is loved. Don't be afraid of hugs and closeness.

24. Get a family calendar and start planning important family activities for three months at a time including family worship time.

25. Start a family night of meaningful and fun family activities. Take turns among the family in choosing places to go and things to do.

26. Begin regular family councils, add them to the family calendar.

27. Guide the children in their preparation for baptism.

28. Write appreciation notes to the children mentioning their positive character traits. Leave them in their rooms or read them at worship time.

For Your Family

Suggested Worship Activities

1. Topic—"An Affirmation of Father."
   Note: Mother should lead out in this worship.
   Song—"The Family of God."
   Needed Materials—Bibles for everyone.
   a. Bible Activity—*Instructions.* The first to find the text reads it and identifies Abraham's good fatherly qualities.
      Gen. 20:17 __________ (prayed)
      Heb. 11:8; Rom. 4:9 ____(had faith)
      Gen. 21:8 __________ (celebrated)
      Rom. 4:3 __________ (believed God)
      Gen. 26:5 __________ (kept commandments)
      Heb. 6:13-15 __________ (had patience)
      John 8:56 __________(rejoiced in Christ)
      Heb. 7:2 __________(paid tithe)
   b. Ellen G. White reading—"Abraham, 'the friend of God,' set us a worthy example. His was a life of prayer. Wherever he pitched his tent, close beside it was set up his altar, calling all within his encampment to the morning and evening sacrifice."—*Patriarchs and Prophets,* p. 128.
   c. Affirmation
      Each family member tells the father those

things he likes about him; or
Family members write a love note to him which they will read at the next worship.

2. Topic—"A Special Day for a Special Dad."

   Note: Mother or an older child should lead in this worship.

   Bible reading—Dan. 7:9.

   a. List ten qualities of the heavenly Father

   1 ____________ 6 ____________
   2 ____________ 7 ____________
   3 ____________ 8 ____________
   4 ____________ 9 ____________
   5 ____________ 10 ____________

   b. Share letter(s) of affirmation with Father—the priest of the family.

   c. Trace the family tree of Terah for five generations (Joshua 24:2-4; Gen. 46:19).

   d. What did the name Abraham mean?________
   ANSWER: *Abram* means "exalted father." *Abraham* means "father of a great multitude."

   e. *Action Plan.* Set up a family committee to have a "His Day" for father. Spend it honoring him. Each person contributes to make the day special for dad.

3. Topic—"God Chose Dad."

   Bible reading—Gen.18:18, 19

   a. Why did God choose Abraham?____________

   b. Why has God chosen the father and priest of our home?

   Ellen G. White reading—*Patriarchs and Prophets,* p. 144:

   "Let the father, as priest of the household, lay upon the altar of God the morning and evening sacrifice, while the wife and children unite in prayer and praise. In such a household Jesus will tarry. . . . From these homes morning and evening prayer ascends to God as sweet incense, and His mercies and blessings descend upon the suppliants like morning dew."

c. We are told that every place Abraham moved his tent he built an altar. "Like the patriarchs of old, those who profess to love God should erect an altar to the Lord wherever they pitch their tent."—*Ibid.*
   Why?________________________________

Standing in the Gap

" 'So I sought for a man among them who would make a wall, and stand in the gap before Me on behalf of the land, that I should not destroy it; but I found no one' " (Eze. 22:30, N.K.J.V.).

"He saw that there was no man, and wondered that there was no intercessor" (Isa. 59:16).

A runner approached, eagerly awaited by the city's leaders. Breathlessly he revealed that thousands of well-armed, fierce tribesmen were headed their way. Fear gripped the council. The city was ill-prepared to withstand such an attack. What could they do to protect their homes, their children, and their city? Even as they debated, a long line of horsemen with swords and spears gleaming in the sunlight appeared over the crest of the mountain north of the city. No more time for argument. Only immediate action could save their capital. "Cut the bridge!" the order went out. Muscles bulged, and sweat poured off the brows of the crew who worked feverishly to destroy the structure. As the axes chewed away at the massive timbers, the men could hear the hoofbeats of the enemy's horses descending the mountain.

Quick! Someone must stand in the gap and defend the narrow bridge so that the axmen could finish their task. Who would go? Horatius rapidly put his armor on. Grabbing his sword and shield, he rushed across the bridge and took his position at its narrow entrance as the enemy assembled.

"Just who does he think he is!" sneered the enemy commander. A roar of laughter echoed from the troops.

The enemy champion proudly strode forward and engaged the defender, only to have a gleaming sword cut him down. Another and yet another dueled with Horatius, who stood his ground. The minutes seemed like hours while the valiant Horatius held thousands of invaders at bay. Then the bridge creaked, shuddered, and finally thundered into the Tiber. Only then did Horatius dive into the current. The water ran red from the soldier's wounds as he strained every fatigued muscle to reach the other side. Weighted by his armor, he would disappear beneath the waves, only to reappear struggling onward. A shout of gratitude and victory arose from the city as he gained the other shore. Rome was saved because someone had been willing to stand in the gap!

The Bible pictures God as desirous of saving the land—the souls of men—but hindered because He can't find someone to stand in the gap. It's as though the enemy were coming in like a flood—the wall has been breached. God is eager to save the city. But He needs a man, a woman, or a child to intercede—to reclaim the ground that others have yielded to the enemy, Satan—and to join Him in His great quest of saving others. " 'So I sought for a man among them who would make a wall, and stand in the gap . . . ; but I found no one' " (Eze. 22:30, N.K.J.V.). God is searching for intercessors today who will provide prayer support for family members and friends during the raging battle between good and evil. He must have someone to stand in the gap!

The Value of Intercessory Prayer

Young children do not understand the issues involved in the struggle between good and evil. But fathers and mothers are custodians over their souls and possess the *right* to intercede for them before God.

But our awesome authority goes beyond "standing

in" for our children. The Christian who claims God as his Father must call every man his brother and kindred. During the cosmic struggle with the evil one, we will note that some of our comrades in arms are sorely beset by the enemy as the conflict rages. Perhaps they are hesitating in the battle or are unsure of the power of their weaponry. We Christians have the privilege of "standing in" for any individual for whom Christ died. That is what intercessory prayer is all about.

Scripture records no less than 105 intercessory prayers. Abraham's intercession would have spared Sodom if the city had contained ten righteous individuals in it (Gen. 18:22-32). Moses "stood . . . in the breach," identifying himself with the sins of the people, and saved the nation when it deserved destruction (Ps. 106:23; Ex. 32:32). Job's three friends were forgiven after he prayed for them (Job 42:8), and Daniel's intercession (Dan. 10:12, 13) brought Christ Himself into the fray to change the mind of the stubborn king of Persia, so that Israel could return to the Promised Land.

In the New Testament Jesus told Peter that Satan was trying to sift him as wheat, but that He had prayed for him that his faith would not fail, and that He had claimed victory for the weak, vascillating disciple (Luke 22:31, 32). Paul was the great apostle of intercession, with almost every Epistle containing examples of intercessory prayer. He saw a power available to the Christian that is "mighty through God to the pulling down of strong holds," "casting down imaginations, . . . and bringing into captivity every thought to the obedience of Christ" (2 Cor. 10:4, 5). Christ intercedes (Heb. 7:25), the Holy Spirit intercedes (Rom. 8:26, 27), and we are to intercede for others (1 Tim. 2:1).

Interceding for Members of the Family

Intercession brings supernatural allies into the battle.

The discouraged and disheartened find new strength and those under bondage to the enemy are freed from their captivity so that they may again have free choice whether they want to serve God or not. Hannah's continuing prayers for Samuel brought supernatural agencies to his side and protected him against the evil influences of Eli's sons. Job offered burnt offerings for all his children "continually" (Job 1:5).

The story of the boy with the dumb spirit illustrates the dynamics involved. Satan had possessed the young lad. The nine disciples could do nothing. Christ appeared and the father implored, "If You can do anything, have compassion on us and help us." Jesus turned the tables on the father and said, "If *you* can believe, all things are possible to him who believes." Notice, *the healing of the son depended on the faith of the father* (see Mark 9:22, 23). The faith of the father permitted Jesus to intervene in favor of a third party. Satan desperately resisted, but finally had to give up his captive.

We had been praying for a certain family for several years. The parents and their grown children scarcely spoke to one another and had severed all social contacts. The married daughter fell ill with cancer and her mother's words to her during a quarrel rang in her ears: "I never want to see you again!" We tried to bridge the gulf to the daughter only to be rebuffed.

One Sabbath afternoon we studied the prophecy of Malachi 4 with the mother, and together knelt in a circle and interceded with tears that God would turn and tune the hearts of the estranged mother and daughter to each other. In faith we claimed God's healing of relationships even though we saw no visible evidence of it.

Sunday morning the mother called us as early as she dared. With joy in her voice she asked, "Do you know who phoned me last night? At 2:00 A.M. my telephone rang and a timid voice on the other end of the line whispered, 'Mother, I love you!' It was our daughter Nelda!" They visited more than an hour, abandoning their longstanding hostilities and forgiving each other. We responded, "Praise the Lord!" and rejoiced with her. Was that call a coincidence? We don't think so. We believe that God directly intervened to answer our intercessory prayer.

We have seen God's hand freed to intervene in the lives of our children. For some time we were concerned about a certain friendship one of our children had. It seemed unhealthy for all concerned. As parents we one day earnestly besought God's intervention. That very week the two broke off the relationship. You could not convince us that God did not act to answer our prayers!

Intercessory prayer makes a difference in home discipline also. One of our relatives shared how her 3-year-old daughter was kicking and carrying on because she didn't want to take her bath. The mother had had a hard day, and the confrontation annoyed her. Suddenly her little girl stopped and said, "Mommy, pray for me." The mother and daughter knelt right beside the bathtub, and the mother prayed for her child. Scarcely had she said Amen when her little one, all smiles, jumped into the tub and took her bath.

When we face a confrontation with our children on any delicate issue, oftentimes I will deal with the issue while Millie retires to another room to intercede in prayer. Repeatedly we have seen the tide turn as supernatural agencies have intervened at these critical points in their lives, and we have praised God together for the victory.

Not long ago I visited a friend who was terribly discouraged about her son's life. He was rebelling at home, at school, and against society. The day before my visit she and her husband felt impressed to come to a meeting at which we spoke on intercession for the family. She repeatedly voiced her surety that the Lord had sent them there for exactly what they needed. Then she confessed, "Things were so bad that I almost gave up on our son."

"You can't," I quickly responded. "That is exactly what Satan would like. You have to fight for him. The battle between good and evil is raging in his life. You must fight in prayer for him."

Then she admitted, "But I don't like to fight. It isn't part of my nature."

Again I came back, "But you have to. You must confront the enemy and lean on the Almighty for strength and for your son's spiritual salvation!" We knelt and I prayed an intercessory battle prayer, and the Lord heard. The next week went much better. Today he is growing spiritually as a young Christian.

Our right to pray for our children does not end the day they leave home. We have the blessed privilege of interceding for them even if they are grown and have families of their own. Here is a promise that John and I continually claim for ourselves, our children, and our future grandchildren when our sons get married. (Fill in the blanks with the names of your family prayer list.)

"This is my covenant with __________, saith the Lord; My spirit is upon __________, and my words which I have put in __________mouth, shall not depart out of __________ mouth, nor out of the mouth of thy seed [__________], nor out of the mouth of thy seed's seed[__________], saith the Lord, from henceforth and forever" (Isa. 59:21).

Recently a group of students in one of our colleges joined in an all-night prayer vigil. Do you know what kind of prayers predominated? The leader told us that she had thought the students would pray for themselves and their own needs, but their greatest concern, it turned out, was the spiritual condition of their parents. Intercessory prayer is not always parents praying for children, but—thank God—many children are also praying their parents through spiritual crises.

While teaching school in Texas, I invited the children to share their prayer requests. A brother and sister would frequently ask that we pray for their father, who did not know the Lord. After several years, one Sabbath evening in an evangelistic meeting the pastor made a call as the choir sang and intercessory prayers ascended to heaven. The father hesitated, but then rose to his feet and walked to the front. This answer to the prayers of a son and a daughter for their father moved the congregation to tears. In emotion the choir stopped singing. Joy filled every heart because another family was moving together toward the kingdom of heaven.

Nothing pleases God more than to have His Word quoted back to Him in prayer and to have His promises claimed in behalf of saving the lost. He delights as in prayer we storm the enemy's strongholds to rescue the captives. God does not propose to force them into heaven against their will, but He does liberate them from bondage so that they can again make a free choice—for God or for Satan. Our prayers authorize God to cross Satan's boundaries and once again intervene in their lives. The Lord can initiate a chain of events which ultimately will lead many (indeed, the vast majority) of them back to Him. This is what it means to be a priest. It is the priesthood of all believers (Ex. 19:6; 1 Peter 2:9)—fathers, mothers, children interceding for one another—praying one another over life's rough places and onward to the kingdom.

"It is a part of God's plan to grant us, in answer to the prayer of faith, that which He would not bestow did we not thus ask."—*The Great Controversy,* p. 525.

With all these heavenly blessings available at our

kneeling place, isn't it strange that we pray so little? Well might the Almighty wonder: "He saw that there was no man, and wondered that there was no intercessor" (Isa. 59:16).

God says, "I gave My life's blood to redeem your son, your daughter, your friend. I can't understand why *you* aren't interceding for your own flesh and kind when I gave My all. Won't *you* stand in the gap?"

Alone With God

" 'Be ready in the morning. . . . Present yourself to me there on top of the mountain. No one is to come with you' " (Ex. 34:2, 3, N.I.V.).

"All who are under the training of God need the quiet hour for communion with their own hearts, with nature, and with God."—The Ministry of Healing, *p. 58.*

"If you don't have personal devotions—forget family worship!" The statement shocked me. Had I heard correctly? We had written queries to some well-known Christian leaders for their insights into family worship. But it was the letter we didn't receive that impressed us most. Morris Venden did not mail a response, but our travels coincided in Costa Rica where we were both scheduled to speak at a Central American ministerial session. When Morris saw us he apologetically said, "Oh, about that letter I owe you. What I have to say about family worship can be said in one sentence. If you don't have personal devotions—forget family worship!"

Initially, I was stunned. Then I began arguing with him in my thoughts. But, Morris, if you don't have personal devotions, you would need family worship even more before beginning the day. In my mind I made two parallel columns: one with reasons why Morris was wrong, and the other with reasons why he *might* be right. The whirling mental gears finally did a total reverse. He's right! I conceded at last. Personal devotions should come first, and family worship can't be a substitute for them.

Reasons for Having Personal Morning Devotions First

1. You can't share what you don't have. The family doesn't want stale bread at the morning feast, but fresh shewbread—warm off the coals of our own communion with God.
2. No priest in the ancient sanctuary would sacrifice for others until he first had obtained cleansing for himself.
3. As we ask for the Holy Spirit in individual worship, He will convict and teach, guiding us on how to present principles that meet the particular needs of family members in worship.
4. If each person has his personal time with the Lord, each will be more "tuned in" and receptive to the corporate family worship experience.

Time-out for Mom

In a baseball game, any player has the right to call for a time-out. However, in the game of life Mom often doesn't *have* any time-out. It is a "given" that her first responsibility is to get husband, children, and frequently herself off to work or school.

Every mother needs her hour with the Lord and has the right to personal devotion time. How else will she be fortified to meet the frustrations of the day and to nurture growing minds with the power of the Holy Spirit? Satan will keep mothers too busy doing *good* things so that he can keep them from doing *better* things. He will even give us a guilt trip when we do put God first, whispering to us that we'd better not let the family down—we'll need more time for breakfast, making lunches, and getting them off.

But stop! Such priority time actually prepares, not robs, an individual for the pressing duties and trials of the day. Many ordeals that otherwise would frustrate us we find swept away when we start the day with the Lord!

From My Diary

My roles as a wife, mother, daughter-in-law, and university teacher present urgent demands on my time. This was one of those days. The peaches were rotting in the baskets. Yellow bugs were eating up the potato plants in the garden. Grandma needed to see the dermatologist, and unexpected company was coming for supper. Wes broke the band on his braces, and so I took him to the orthodontist. And then I had classes to prepare, lectures, committees, and the Rogerses had come by to ask for help because things weren't going well in their marriage.

Years ago it seemed I had more time. As a single person, I routinely spent an hour a day in prayer and reading the Bible or Ellen White. But then the tempo picked up. Conflicting demands began squeezing out that precious part of my day—the doctoral classes, building a new house (trying to decide on green or gold carpets), while I also had to choose between being a Miss or Mrs.

A terrific courtship and fantastic marriage filled my life with excitement and activity. Since John was a widower and father of two energetic sons ages 11 and 12, everything for me had changed at once. In one year I earned the Ed.D., MRS., and two MA MA degrees!

I'd always considered myself to be a caring person. In fact, John mentioned that he was attracted to me because I was caring and thoughtful of others. Students always waited at my door asking for help. But was I still that same person in my new roles? Cooking for five mouths (Grandma was with us) was different from cooking for one. Not used to my new time limitations, one summer I took on a heavy overload of classes, independent studies, M.A. projects, and workshops, trying to please everyone. It was too much for me.

The time pressures from my multiple roles began bringing out hostilities in me I hadn't known were there. I didn't like myself.

It seems like I'd been playing god without God's power—trying to save all marriages and homes; teach classes; conduct workshops; be a perfect wife; an ideal mother; and a farmer's wife with gardening-canning-freezing projects to help the family finances! I felt like it was "Run, run, oh, see Millie run . . . !" Only Millie wasn't getting anywhere!

One evening after a nerve-racking day with the kids at home when the demands of others in my world were too much, the Lord and I had a confrontation.

"Tonight, Lord, I'm too exhausted to sleep. My heart is beating fast, and I am hyper knowing so much has to be done tomorrow. John is on a trip and I'm at my wit's end with the kids, who need us both. I'm tired, frustrated, and discouraged—just running circles. Is this all there is—speeding but only spinning? Trying to help the sons grow in favor with God and man, while the progress seems slow at times? Do You want me to keep serving others, with no time for myself or for devotions? Is that what You intend? It seems I'm trying to save the world alone. I must be doing things on my own which You never intended me to do. Lord, what do You want of me? I submit my life to You—to change. I want more time with You. Speak to me, Lord. Show me what is essential. Take control of my life. I'm sure doing a bad job of it myself." Finally, in the early hours of the morning, sleep came.

From the Doldrums to Meaning

It would be impressive to tell you that an angel spoke to me, that "I heard a voice say . . . ," but nothing that dramatic happened. Nonetheless, that was the beginning of a new and closer walk with the Lord. That day I hung a poster on the refrigerator, "Slow me down, Lord." He began to open my eyes to some of my motives for hurrying: unholy ambition, pride, and hostility. Determination surged within me. My morning devotional time became sacred and meaningful. I began to have more peace and calmness in my life. John and I discovered new ways to study the Bible. Other changes came. We were invited to a prayer fellowship with three God-fearing, loving couples which led us into new frontiers with Jesus Christ.

As we wrestled in our prayer time with our duties and calling, strange things began to happen. A few days before we were to fly to an out-of-State Marriage Commitment Seminar we were to conduct, the telephone rang. "We're so embarrassed, but the seminar just hasn't filled and we'll have to cancel," the voice on it said. "That's all right," I answered. "We understand. Please don't feel bad." With the phone back on the hook, John and I joyfully hugged each other and said, "Praise the Lord!" Then a couple called whom we had been counseling. She had a new job, things were going better, and they wouldn't be able to keep their Tuesday evening appointment. Other appointments fell through. The chairman of the education department summoned me and gently probed, "Millie, I'm afraid you're working too hard. What can I do to help lighten the load?"

The crisis passed, and now the Lord is giving me new, exciting insights in my personal devotions. I pray that God will focus my energies on the most important items of *His* agenda for me. I don't want to "run aimlessly," or to box "as one beating the air" (1 Cor. 9:26, R.S.V.). I'm totally committed to take time out alone with God so that "God's program shall prosper in [my] hands" (Isa. 53:10, T.L.B.).

Senseless Stampede Versus God's Prosperous Program

We find that the day, like the proverbial bull, must be caught by the horns. Otherwise it begins with a roaring rush and ends in dire disaster. And we've all experienced that disaster. Let's look at a typical situation. Mother gets up and dresses. She realizes it's late so she says a quick prayer and maybe reads a text, promising herself, "I'll take time for Bible study and prayer tonight." Then she hurries to fix breakfast, squeezing in the preparation of lunches between answering phone calls and helping the children to find misplaced clothes. While she is getting ready for "the Exodus," Father is trying to get the income tax paper completed before going to the office. At the appropriate (or inappropriate) time, he calls for a short and to-the-point family worship. The kids start crawling in, after the third call. George can't seem to finish a lengthy telephone discussion with his friend Jack on how to solve the algebra problem on page eighty-two.

Father, with furrows of tension marking his face, again calls the family. "Now let's hurry up so we can have worship! Cut it, George. Sit up, Dave. Mary, stop playing with the cat." It doesn't quite sound like "What a Fellowship, What a Joy Divine!" does it?

The time to get started is the evening before. Biblically the day begins at sunset. This makes sense. A family evening, a winding down of the pace, and an early bedtime, will prepare the family emotional climate and health for the duties of the coming daylight hours. It will recharge the emotional and spiritual batteries. The late-night TV show has torpedoed daylight hours of many a day. Now we try to begin the day right by getting to bed early in a peaceful frame of mind, with major priorities set for the next day. If you don't make plans the night before, the early-morning communion with God is likely to be squeezed out and the family, like a herd of stampeding cattle, will be running toward they know not what.

As we write this, we try to cut off work about 7:00 or 8:00 P.M. Ellen White has encouraged us not to continue the business of the day into the evening. Longfellow said that between the hour of dusk and sleep there is a time which he called "the children's hour." The evening really *should* be "family time," when we can develop meaningful relationships. Usually we cut off the phones about eight o'clock so that we can retire between nine and ten and rise about 5:00 or 5:30 A.M. for our personal devotions.

The first thing we do in the morning is to praise God and choose Him to be the Lord and Saviour of our lives and of our children's for the day. We invite the Holy Spirit to guide us, and we ask for His wisdom and good judgment in all we do. John commits our family to the Lord, putting us under God's protective umbrella. Then we release our sons to God for Him to do for them that which we cannot do. The "blood is put on the doorposts" through prayer, and we believe God's angels then watch over our home. Finally we have our individual devotions.

John and I do enjoy these personal devotions in our "private closets," which are in separate parts of the house since it is difficult for me to resist the urge to interrupt him and share some choice quotation I've just discovered or to ask him a historical-philosophical question that my study has provoked. We find it better to share *after* our individual worship time. Also, we have greater freedom for kneeling, writing, talking, or even crying unto the Lord, when we are *alone* on our mountain of prayer.

At 6:00 A.M. we have worship with one son who must be to work by six-thirty, and then we continue our private quiet time until seven o'clock, when we splash into the Andrews University swimming pool. Some may prefer to jog or take a morning walk. One is thus energized for the day's activities—both spiritually and physically.

Family Worship—Not a Ceremony, but a Lifestyle

Once we published a list of ninety-six family altar suggestions. The list made the rounds and I suppose it did some good. But even if we expanded the list to 1,096 hints, it might never save our families. In many families worship isn't going anywhere, because the whole lifestyle is out of step with God's plan. If worship isn't a vital experience, we need to take a long look at our way of life, priorities, and the pace of existence. A few band-aids will not suffice if major surgery is necessary.

A friend confided to us, "For the first fifty years of my life I thought the secret of success was work, work, work. I've discovered that I had my priorities wrong. The secret of success is pray, pray, pray!" Do our families need to think of living a simpler life with more time for prayer? If family worship doesn't fit into our lives,why doesn't it?

Are we decided that we won't settle for anything short of God's best? And are we willing to place everything on God's altar to be retained or given up as His providence shall indicate? If in our particular situation God's best might conceivably mean a change of jobs, a move out of the city to a more simple life, or a radical revamp of a swamped schedule—would we be willing to pay the price? God's rich reward is that we will receive a hundredfold in this life . . . and in the kingdom to come, eternal life!

David said, "My voice shalt thou hear in the morning, O Lord; in the morning will I direct my prayer unto thee, and will look up" (Ps. 5:3). God told Moses, "Be ready in the morning. . . . Present yourself to me there on . . . the mountain. No one is to come with you" (Ex. 34:2, 3, N.I.V.).

Alone with God! What greater honor could there be! As we come out of our mountain, our faces will shine and our hearts will burn within us. Angels' wings will dissipate the clouds of darkness which would have surrounded our feet. Then as we gather around the altar together, the promise of Isaiah will be fulfilled, "All thy children shall be taught of the Lord; and great shall be the peace of thy children."

They Too Will Stand Alone

"We need not fear that our children will stand tall before man if they have bowed low before God."

Little Sulvig was only 8 and her sister Christa was 6. As the people gathered in the meetinghouse, they could see small groups huddling in the corners. Cautiously Sulvig drew a little closer and strained her ears to try to hear what the big people were whispering about. "Brother Olafson was thrown into jail today," one adult said, "and the town officials say that any man or woman who publicly preaches, against the teachings of the state church, that Jesus is coming soon will be immediately imprisoned."

It was time for the meeting to begin. As the people took their seats, a policeman entered and sat in the last pew. Sulvig noted glances passing between her daddy, who was deacon, and the elder of the church. No one moved. It was so quiet that she thought she could hear her own heart beating. She could see her mother's lips moving though her eyes were closed. Her mother must have been praying. After a bit someone began to sing and everyone joined in, but no one dared to speak.

Suddenly Sulvig found herself walking to the platform. Who was that by her side? It was Christa. Sulvig began to speak—not that she wanted to talk. Somehow it seemed that it was as if Jesus and the angels were speaking through her. The girl wasn't afraid. The people strained their necks trying to see her, but Daddy came to the rescue and set her and Christa on top of the table. All the texts that she had learned seemed to just roll out.

They were the very same promises she had heard in family worship. Without fear she told the people that Jesus was coming soon. Her sister, who couldn't even read yet, spoke out against the drinking of alcohol. Sulvig watched as the town drunk fell to his knees, pleading, "God, be merciful to me, a sinner." Others also began to call to God for mercy, and a Mr. Johnson, who had stolen something from her daddy years before, crossed the aisle and with tears in his eyes said he was sorry. Everybody looked happy now, except the policeman who turned pale. Suddenly he got up and left. Sulvig felt good that even though the big people couldn't say anything, God had spoken through her lips and had shared the good news that Jesus was coming soon.

History records this method of spreading the gospel during the 1840s in the Scandinavian countries. When the law prohibited men and women from preaching, the Holy Spirit came upon young children who then proclaimed the message. Will this ever happen again? Ellen White tells us:

"In the closing scenes of this earth's history many of these children and youth will astonish people by their witness to the truth, which will be borne in simplicity, yet with spirit and power. They have been taught the fear of the Lord, and their hearts have been softened by a careful and prayerful study of the Bible. In the near future many children will be endued with the Spirit of God, and will do a work in proclaiming the truth to the world, that at that time cannot well be done by the older members of the church."—*Counsels to Parents and Teachers*, pp. 166, 167.

How Can We Encourage Children to Pray?

One reason why children haven't learned to pray seriously is that many of them have lived such sheltered, adventureless lives that they find nothing urgent to pray about. An early meaningful prayer experience of one of our sons came in a moment of extremity in the northern woods.

John junior paddled with a J-stroke while I sat in the front of the canoe studying the map. "You'll find the outlet of this lake over to the right beyond that point," I told him. "Oh, oh, it looks like we're going to have to portage around some waterfalls—and before we hit the stretch going up into Ivanhoe Provincial Park, we're going to have to portage two miles! I feel tired already!"

It was great country. We had traveled a day and a half without seeing another human being in the vast Canadian woods. It was a man's adventure that took every ounce of energy and ingenuity we could muster. While inching the canoe down some rapids by rope, we swamped out (overturned), and if 14-year-old John junior had not done the work of two or three, our seventeen-foot canoe might be wrapped around some rock in the Ontario rapids today. Then came the long portage. Moved with insane enthusiasm, we decided to carry the canoe and the whole load in one trip. Looking at the map, I saw we would cross several streams, and so to lighten the load, I poured out all the drinking water. After struggling overland for a mile, we felt that the creases made by the aluminum crosspieces on our aching shoulders might be getting indelible. We panted up to the first creek and found it dry. Another half hour of agony and we arrived at the second creek. It too was dry! Our tongues seemed swollen and every cell in our bodies cried out for water.

Sitting on the rocky bank, I leaned against a log. Why had I risked pouring out all our water? Meanwhile John junior explored up the creek. On his hands and knees, he peered down between the rocks. Yes, he could see the reflection of water down there. He could even hear it trickling! But he had no way to get it. Immediately he prayed, "Lord, I'm terribly thirsty. You've said that we should call on You when we're in trouble. Help me find some way to get a drink of water. In Jesus' name, Amen." Then he opened his eyes and looked around. Right beside him was a tall, slender, dry weed. He cut it with his knife, snipped the top off it as well, and threaded it down between the rocks. It was a natural straw. He drank, and I drank. That night on the shores of the next lake we had worship, let the embers of our campfire burn low, and then sat transfixed as God put on His show. The great northern lights unrolled, shimmered, and danced across the heavens. We'll never forget that day. In our family museum we still preserve the natural "straw" we used to drink water on that dry, dusty trek. And we still preserve in our memories the surety that youths' extremities are God's opportunities to instill habits of trust in a faithful heavenly Father who is able to meet all their needs.

Praying and Witnessing on Their Own

As parents we should avoid one-way family worships, but rather find ways of involving the children as active participants in the experience. We want them to catch the worship habit like the measles with two results: (1) that they will pray, witness, and have their own devotions, and (2) that they will be prepared to continue creative family worships in their own homes as they mature, become independent, and marry. How can we guide children toward such habits?

While ministering in Hawaii we were guests in a certain home on one of the islands. The daughter cheerfully gave us her room for two nights during our visit. Among the things that impressed us about the room was not only the neatness, but a chart apparently prepared by her mother. I can't recall exactly what it had on it, but it went something like this:

7:30—Rise, prayer, personal devotions
Wash face and hands, dress
Make bed and tidy room
7:55—Worship and breakfast time
Help clean up in kitchen
8:30—Leave for school
3:30—Play time; outdoor activities,
read good books, or play games
4:00—Practice piano
4:30—Home duties, fold clothes and other assigned duties;
Then free time
6:00—Dinner and help clean up
6:45—Worship
7:00—Homework
9:45—Study Sabbath school lesson and have own evening prayer
10:00—Lights out

I was delighted with the daily schedule for the daughter. What I like most was the time set for individual prayer, Sabbath school lesson study, and family worship.

Some youth have not been taught from an early age to have their individual worship. Yet as teenagers they should be encouraged to do so. A mother once asked, "How can you get your teens to have their own devotions? As a family, we have our morning and evening time with singing, praying, and reading the devotional book or the Bible, but no way can I get my teenagers to have personal devotions. 'Oh, Mom,' they complain, 'twice a day is enough! Besides in school we have worship again.' "

Making personal Bible study and prayer a habit for life is desirable for parents and children alike. Our two sons are just as normal as other Seventh-day Adventist children, so I won't paint halos over their heads. They are all American/Chilean boys (both born in Chile) who have their ups and downs. When they were younger we often encouraged them to have their private time with the Lord. We've told them, "When you have your own devotions, we don't worry so much about you."

Children start this meaningful experience with the Lord at different ages. Some never find the need. It may be a trial or difficulty that causes some to enjoy the prayer and study time, or perhaps a teacher spurring them on to find a more meaningful life. Somehow a nucleus spark ignites. Do you remember when you first started having your personal devotions? What was your motivating factor?

When our boys were about 12 and 13 years of age, we acquired stronger convictions that they should each have their own personal devotions. We stretched our minds to come up with some ingenious technique for inspiring them to get into the habit of reading their Bibles, studying their Sabbath school lesson, and kneeling for prayer. Somehow we wanted them to develop a consistent habit.

As parents we don't always know what spiritual growth is developing behind the teenager's closed door, and often we fear the worst. Sometimes we're wrong. Millie and I observed indications of Bible reading and some underlined Sabbath school quarterlies. John junior tried maintaining his skills in Spanish by reading the Spanish Bible, but was it a consistent habit? Was he growing spiritually or just practicing the language? We tried several behavioral modification tricks of paying them five cents for each chapter read or 25 cents for any good book finished. For a time we encouraged everyone to have personal devotions before morning worship and then share in family worship. That sort of fizzled. Then we all read our Sabbath school quarterlies silently together at the beginning of morning worship, but that too just wasn't natural and didn't work. Finally we decided that we wouldn't force them in personal devotion habits, but we could encourage them.

If at a very early age the home has a sustained silent period when everyone, including the children, goes to a private place for individual spiritual celebration, there is a greater probability that the practice will continue in adulthood. We may lead small children gently and sequentially, with materials appropriate for their age and development.

One family has a special corner of a room for their young children's devotional place, complete with picture books and activities for the child who can't read and easy books and materials for the little one just learning. The mother has outlined steps for their personal devotions and spiritual instruction. During these special moments, they not only read the Sabbath school lessons, but memorize verses and learn stories to later share with their mother in a feedback session. While they are doing this, Mother is having her quiet time nearby just in case the children need her assistance. At the close she asks, "Do you have any questions I can help you with?" Then the mother and children proceed to dialog in search of Bible answers.

In another home the parents of 2- and 4-year-olds use the flannel board to tell the morning family worship story. The flannel pictures remain on the easel and the children play worship throughout the day, retelling the story to each other. That evening they share it with Father and Mother. True, they distort some of the facts, but little minds are learning and growing!

You can make tapes of the Sabbath school stories and include Your Story Hour tapes or records as part of the child's individual Bible corner. The child can even have his own earphones, so that the parents can still enjoy their quiet time. With all that the Sabbath School

Department is producing, individual worship for the little ones is an increasing reality. Memory verse song tapes and supplementary materials are available and children enjoy them. The important purpose is to help the child make personal devotions a habit, and gradually remove his or her dependency on the parents.

Daring to Be a Daniel

Daniel was but a lad when abruptly removed from familiar surroundings and taken against his will by an alien army to Babylon. There a pagan court urged all its allurements and corruptions on him. No father or mother could check on him, and, indeed, strict obedience to God might well cost him his life in the new surroundings. But Daniel had learned as a child to think for himself. He undoubtedly experienced his own prayer life and personal devotions. "Daniel purposed in his heart that he would not defile himself" (Dan. 1:8).

"Many a lad of today, growing up as did Daniel in his Judean home, studying God's word and His works, and learning the lessons of faithful service, will yet stand in legislative assemblies, in halls of justice, or in royal courts, as a witness for the King of kings."—*Education,* p. 262.

Our children may well have to stand alone. Let's prepare them by encouraging them in their personal devotions and prayer life!

How to Transmit a Heritage

"Unless we have mothers like Elisabeth and Mary today, it will be difficult to have children like John the Baptist and Jesus Christ."

"All I need is a garage to park my car in, a closet to store my wardrobe in, a full refrigerator, and a microwave," someone has said. Today's society pretends that the day-care center will socialize the young child, school will instruct him, the community will entertain him, and the government will give him his old-age pension and bury him.

Will this transmit a heritage? The Christian religion is always only one generation from extinction—as endangered a species as the whooping crane or California condor in our all-pervasive, fast-moving culture. Ideals do not live on simply because they are great or true—they survive only when implanted in the lives and characters of the children and youth. Where does the home come in? How can we make it a relay to pass on the torch of truth to the following generation?

Once the home assumed the primary responsibilities of most of life's valued activities. Work centered in the home. It was an economic unit where parents and children labored together to survive. People were born at home, cared for their aged there, and died in it surrounded by loved ones. Home was the original school, the first church, the main entertainment center. But in the last decades of the twentieth century, for many it is only a filling station.

Why should the *home* transmit the heritage? Because

it is primarily responsible for the religious education and values formation of the younger generation. While the advanced technological society may require us to substitute certain functions elsewhere, this dimension cannot be transferred—its responsibility is nonnegotiable.

Family interaction is vital in transmitting the religious heritage. Some specific goals we can best meet through personal interaction and conversation, working and playing together. But it takes planning to utilize these opportunities. Planning allows us to fulfill the unique needs of each child. Family worship becomes an integration point and a forum where planning can happen.

Why Do We Have Family Worship?

God's plan is that Christian families stop all activities morning and evening and recognize the living God in song, praise, Bible reading, and prayer. The short service becomes a special fellowship time when the Holy Spirit and angels bring the divine Presence into our homes, resulting in peace and increased family harmony. It is the time of the morning and evening sacrifice, a time when spiritual instruction can take place.

Some feel that an elaborately planned program is essential. However, this is not necessary. Simplicity marks all God's activities. But this doesn't mean lack of preparation. We get things ready beforehand for work, recreation, parties, and meals, but what about worship? Is it supposed to turn out well with little or no planning? Ellen White tells us, "To make such a service what it should be, thought should be given to preparation"—*Education,* p. 186. Many of us have been guilty of doing nothing more than grabbing a book as we rush to ring the worship bell.

Usually we may read and discuss one or two verses

from the Bible, sing a stanza of hymn, and repeat a short prayer. Such recognition of God in worship takes only five to ten minutes. There's no necessity to make it long and complicated unless perhaps once or twice a week one desires to spend extra time on religious instruction or celebration. If the children do not attend church school, the parents may wish to teach them daily, perhaps from the same textbooks used in our parochial schools. This may require some additional preparation time.

How to Assess Needs

When educators plan a school curriculum for students they often perform a "needs assessment." They investigate what students know or don't know, and evaluate their attitudes, studying potential improvements. The parents, in the home, can also conduct a simple needs assessment on their family.

In our home when we were praying that our young sons would grow in favor with God and man, we would often take Sunday morning to do a family needs assessment. We would start by making two columns of plusses and minuses for the strengths and weaknesses of each boy. It helped us become more aware of needs, and motivated us to plan instruction to meet them. It also guided us in choosing our prayer and worship topics.

After assessing needs, we wrote an action plan and listed our goals. The plans included the preparation of worship topics, individual talks, friendly family chats, and prayer that God would lead others to teach our children in a way that would reinforce home instruction. Informal table talk took care of some of these topics. Others we discussed while pulling weeds, riding to the dentist's office, or cleaning up after dinner. Always we searched for God's guidance in instructing in the spirit of the great Biblical model found in Deuteronomy 6:7-9:

"You shall teach them diligently to your children, and shall talk of them when you sit in your house, and when you walk by the way, and when you lie down, and when you rise. . . . You shall write them on the doorposts of your house and on your gates" (R.S.V.).

Nothing written before or since has surpassed this instruction on nurturing children. But notice before we can present God's will to our children, the preceding verses remind us, "*You* shall love the Lord your God with all your heart, with all your soul, and with all your might. And these words which I command you today shall be in your heart" (verses 5, 6, N.K.J.V.). Although we have failed many times, we have attempted, by God's grace, to model the Christian life and teach it by incidental bits and pieces in small doses to our sons.

Preparation is important, for if parents do not make any, how can we determine goals, let alone reach them? The children will grow up like untrained vines in the vineyard, with no fruit. But God will richly reward our efforts to pinpoint needy areas and in asking Him for specific results.

In the beginning, we didn't ask the boys to participate in our family-needs assessment. But as they grew older, we could talk about our family weaknesses as a whole, extending the assessment list to include all of us. Wes had a concern about the physical fitness of the family. When his turn came to lead in worship, what do you suppose his topics were? Exercise, fresh air, and diet! Then the family would start jogging again, cut down on sweets, and try to live more balanced lives.

The family-needs assessment permits you to customize family worship and instruction. Since every family is different, the results will vary. They may call for more participation of parents in family fun activities, temperate living, improving communication skills, sibling unity, character training, guiding the finances, positive use of time, or changes in social behavior.

Should the negative or weakness aspect of your family be anger, then let the family read what God says about this emotion and search for the reasons why you become angry in the family. Then in family council look for ways of solving problems that cause anger in the home. Perhaps the family needs to become acquainted with some of the skill-building books that deal with communications and conflict.

One ground rule is that no worship be conducted on threatening topics that would produce resentment because of the current situation. We don't come to worship to "club" one another with inspired writings, but gather in a common search to discover and then follow the will of God as a family. Worship is not the place for disciplinary action or laying down laws. Leave that for family council or, better yet, for individual counseling time. For us, we found that nonthreatening topics such as happiness, pride, positive attitude, jealousy, love for others, communication, fear, helping, doing our best, et cetera, were more appropriate for our worships. Other problem areas required special handling.

A second ground rule is *develop family strengths, rather than harping on weaknesses.* If the difficulty is anger, then extol the value of peace, and search for ways of expressing it in the home life. Emphasize the trait which is the *opposite* of the problem. The Bible says, "Be not overcome of evil, but overcome evil with good" (Rom. 12:21), so build on strengths, rather than haranguing the weaknesses. Accentuate the positive!

Discovering Interests

An interest inventory will provide the tools for the parents to meet the needs discovered by the assessment. If you find your child enjoys nature, use butterflies, bees, or other animals to develop needed spiritual lessons.

Christ used many object lessons from nature and daily life. It may require more preparation, but the time spent will be rewarding for the total family. When our boys were learning about birds in biology class, we often read in worship about birds and their habits, searching for lessons that God has for us through these creatures.

Suppose Freddie is interested in mountain climbing. Plan a family outing up into the mountains, and end the day with a worship around the campfire. Tell a story about mountain climbing—perhaps that of Mallory and Irvine who in the 1920s were last seen by spyglass from a base camp as they approached the summit of the world's highest mountain, Mount Everest. We will never know in this life what befell them, but we do know that they died climbing. What is the hardest mountain to climb? It is Mount Calvary—the giving up of selfish ambitions and sacrificing ourselves for others. Describe how Jesus climbed that mountain. Will there be mountains in heaven? Describe how we can climb, or fly if we prefer, up Mount Zion! "Higher than the highest human thought can reach is God's ideal for His children."—*Education,* p. 18. Do you think that such a worship might have a strong influence in Freddie's life?

It requires some time to plan an interest-oriented worship, but the rewards are thrilling. If the father doesn't have the necessary time, perhaps the mother could research some of the materials. She can file away appropriate stories and nature nuggets. With prayerful preparation, the Holy Spirit will guide.

Everyone Has a Turn

Although the father (as priest of the family) ordinarily leads the worship, we must remember that the Bible teaches the priesthood of *all believers.* Thus the mother and children are also priests and should have their turn to minister to the rest of the family. In our home Daddy

John will occasionally announce, "John Jr., you have worship on Monday night, Wes on Tuesday, and Mom on Thursday." This gains the participation of all and assures variety in the worship experience. Once when my turn came to lead, I gave everyone a card and pencil and asked them each to write all the letters of the alphabet in a vertical column. Then I asked them to write a characteristic of God or to give another word representing God for each letter. After three minutes, we shared our findings and I read a text on the Godhead. Everybody enjoyed the participation, and we enjoyed the unusual and creative thoughts of the boys.

In one home the children traditionally plan the Friday and Sabbath evening worships. All week they search for something special for Friday evening and during the Sabbath hours they are occupied planning a special dress-up pantomime of Bible stories or charades for Sabbath evening. They bring to the worship such joy and creativity that I am sure it causes even the angels to smile.

One weekend two families with children the same ages spent the Sabbath afternoon preparing their worship activity by writing a script on a Bible character. They presented it with costumes, props, and all. The parents recorded it so that they could share it with others later. Lots of giggles and laughter "made memories" of a beautiful Sabbath afternoon.

Resources and Materials

If you need stories, your greatest resources are the experiences of your own childhood and life. Children never tire of hearing of God's protection in our own lives, His answers to our childhood (or adulthood) prayers, or experiences from our travels. When John goes on business trips he returns replenished with special stories and providential experiences. So that he will not forget them, he frequently records them on a 4 by 6 card. I also enjoy collecting material and have a special notebook where I file experiences, creative ideas, and stories for future family worships.

As we search for materials and collect the resources, we should consider the age and development of each child. In families with a spectrum from tiny children to teenagers, parents need to approach the matter with creative wisdom. Our friends Warren and Carolyn supplement the general worship time with individual reading of stories and Sabbath school lessons to the little ones as they tuck them into bed. It isn't easy, and as struggling parents we do not always bat a thousand! The Sabbath school lessons furnish excellent resource material. In *Counsels on Sabbath School Work,* page 41, Ellen White suggests that we should set time aside each day for the study of the Sabbath school lesson with the children. As they grow older, we should encourage them to study their own Sabbath school lesson.

Even interruptions and late arrivals can become resources for special worships. Some of the best heart-to-heart talks we've experienced resulted from having prayer and Bible reading with a son who unavoidably came home too late for our regular worship. When we are faithful as well as flexible, God can take advantage of the irregular situations and turn them into some of the best communication times.

The Adventist Book Center and other religious bookstores have tremendous resources for religious instruction. Parents can obtain flannelgraph materials, games, tapes, stories, quizzes, and enrichment resources recommended by the General Conference Sabbath School Department to supplement the Sabbath school lesson. With all these delightful materials, worship time has become, in many homes, the most fun time of the day.

Music is a most helpful resource to encourage the participation of all in praising God. The purchase of enough songbooks—one for each person—is an important investment. We like to sing the same song several days until we have learned it by memory. Some parents create a family music band, each child having his own instrument. One night of the week can be their "concert" time. I have visited in a home where all the children of the large family played one or more instruments. On Friday and Sabbath evening they all blended their talents in praising the Lord. Every now and again a wrong note floated aimlessly, causing a giggle or two, but it was a joyful experience for both participants and listeners.

Heart-tuning

The most important preparation for worship involves the *heart*. Have you noticed that we profit little from the worship experience if we hold anger in our hearts or unresolved misunderstandings? Many find it meaningful to settle their problems in order to have a heartfelt evening worship.

A couple with serious marital problems went to a counselor for help. After discussing their difficulties, the Christian counselor asked, "Do you two have family worship together?" The response was No. The counselor then asked if they would read a devotional book if she gave it to them, which they agreed to do. Months passed, and the couple didn't return for further counseling. Sometime later the three met on the street, and the counselor asked how things were going. They replied, "Great! The devotional book did it! It never seemed right to have worship when we were upset with each other, so we made it a practice when we had a misunderstanding to reconcile before our morning or evening worship." After twenty-five years, they are still happily married.

Asking forgiveness is a heart preparation. It may be that individuals need to bow before the Lord and say "I'm sorry" to God and perhaps to each other. Much healing comes in the words "I'm sorry; will you forgive me?" I've had to do this and found it difficult, but so essential for restoring relationships not only with God but with the family.

As parents we form the living link between the providential leadings of God in the past and the glorious future of victory which opens up before our children. We cannot transmit to them what has not become a part of our own heart's experience. As the example of our own lives supports our systematic and sustained instruction, the God who has made us all that we are will work powerfully on the lives of our children. The heritage will be transmitted and our family will be a living witness to the greatness of our Lord and Saviour.

Sparking Up the Family Altar

"It only takes a spark to set a fire going."

Call to Worship

A relative visited a missionary family in the tropics. When the family had moved from the jungle to the capital, they had brought with them a pet parrot. As it got close to worship time, he would call, "Ding! Ding! Ding!" mimicking the family's traditional worship bell. The parrot testified, to the guest, of the regularity with which this family priest brought his wife and children together for prayer. And even though the time is designated for this special event of the day, the family still needs to be summoned in some manner from other activities.

In Mexico we picked up an antique bell, which we rang each morning to call the family. Curley Dog always came first. She knew that Wes would feed her when he came into the family room, and she was as conditioned to the bell as Pavlov's dogs. The bell brought the perfect response—time with the boys and the dog. Later, however, our sons informed us that the harsh clanging sound so early in the morning jangled their nerves, and they didn't like it anymore. The same is true of a loud voice yelling "Wor-r-r-ship!" How much nicer to have someone play the piano, a specific record, or to designate a quiet-voiced person to announce the gathering. It's a moment when the earthly family joins the heavenly one in adoration, thanksgiving, and study, and the way we start sets the tone for all the activities that follow.

The family should agree on the best time for the worship hour. With a set schedule, each can plan his other activities accordingly. It may not be fair to expect everyone to come "right now" without warning and could cause negative feelings in the children. One teenager remarked, "I don't mind worship, but since I'm so busy, I'd like to know that it will start and end at a set time, so I can plan." A set time takes away the insecurity of the unknown, and if the father doesn't call worship on time, it can upset the whole family's schedule. Regularity of this part of the daily routine also creates an impression of the importance we attach to it.

Ellen White suggests worship twice a day. "Fathers and mothers, each morning and evening gather your children around you, and in humble supplication lift the heart to God for help."—*Testimonies,* vol. 7, p. 44.

The ideal time for evening worship is the sunset hour, but some homes may find this impossible. One may not have returned from work, another may come in famished—more interested in physical food than in spiritual food. And so, many families designate a compatible hour. If they have little tots, it needs to be around six o'clock or soon after suppertime. Our sons also like to have evening worship following the meal. It seems to extend the fellowship time, and sharing the day's activities provides a break before getting back to their studies.

A brief and to-the-point worship can be more effective than one long and drawn out. John and I have noticed, however, that although the sons prefer short worships when we are in charge, theirs often last fifteen or twenty minutes. It isn't the quantity, but the quality that we remember. Even if the family reads only a few verses, but understands them, the members can experience a real blessing. Ellen White says, "Let the services be brief and full of life."—*Education,* p. 186. Once when the White family was in a rush, it seemed that they didn't have time for worship. However, James White insisted that they have it, and he read a Bible chapter. He chose Psalm 117, the shortest chapter of the Bible—just two verses long.

Sometimes a spiritual serendipity experience will occur. The participants will feel an unexpected outpouring of the Holy Spirit, and each will want to linger in His presence. When one senses the deep moving of the Holy Spirit, he will want to let His agenda take priority over other time appointments.

Dropping the morning and evening worship is an easy thing to do, especially when schedule conflicts crop up. One professional working mother who was married to a physician and had two teenagers in college asked, "What can a family do when everyone's schedule just doesn't synchronize?" We've discovered that it is one of our problems also. Let's look at it. First, the family must decide that it truly wants to control the morning schedule. We asked our college sons to avoid registering for 7:30 A.M. classes, and we would not schedule appointments before eight-fifteen. However, when our youngest took a 6:30 A.M. job we had to make adjustments again. We rise in time to have worship with him at six o'clock. Each quarter we have to reevaluate the schedule.

True, on occasions someone is tardy or absent, but the rest of the family proceeds as scheduled. If the priest of the family is going to be absent, he assigns the function to another person.

For families that must scatter at different times in the morning, one could leave the devotional book out for all to read, and then everyone can discuss it in the evening. This is a little difficult, but possible. The father may even prepare a tape for the family. Frequently mothers take the worship hour when the father has an early departure. Some dads have had such a strong conviction that they should be present for morning worship that they have actually switched jobs. Their particular employment and accompanying lifestyle didn't permit them to provide the family the priority that they felt it deserves. My own husband changed his work three times for the good of the family.

Our worship hour is a heavenly occasion when we are not alone. Ellen White says: "Let the members of every family bear in mind that they are closely allied to heaven. The Lord has a special interest in the families of His children here below. Angels offer the smoke of the fragrant incense for the praying saints. Then in every family let prayer ascend to heaven both in the morning and at the cool sunset hour, in our behalf presenting before God the Saviour's merits. Morning and evening the heavenly universe take notice of every praying household."—*Child Guidance,* p. 519.

Ideas for Family Worship

The telephone rang in our mountain hideout just as we started writing this section. Idalmi, calling from hundreds of miles away, told us she had just read our articles on family worship. She continued that she liked the fact we went beyond the mere identification of the problems in Seventh-day Adventist homes and offered suggestions as well. That is the specific purpose for this section: to present some problem-solving ideas for the family altar.

Idalmi also shared with us that her 9-year-old son and 11-year-old daughter will not go to bed without evening worship. At times when her husband has been away in the evening and she has fallen asleep from exhaustion on the couch, her children—not wanting to disturb her—look for a storybook on their own level they can read for their worship. Then they have prayer together and go to bed! The angels must delight in such moments of adoration and praise which ascend as fragrant incense to the Lord.

Now for some creative ideas. The sky is the limit (or should we say that heaven is the limit?), for certainly the Holy Spirit is the director of worship activities. We have some general suggestions for conducting worship, ways of using the Bible and also the Ellen G. White books, enhancing worship and praising God with music and poetry, and activities or strategies that bring in greater involvement of the participants. After you have tried some of the ideas given, you can make adaptations, and later you can develop your family's own creative ways of worshiping the Lord.

Use of the Bible

First we suggest that we stop reading the Bible. Yes, you read correctly! Stop reading or hearing the Bible and start *studying* it with the family. Reading is only a passive experience. The final and most important part of the learning process is actualization—transferring the message into living reality by asking ourselves, "How would my life change if I actually lived what this verse is talking about?"

The Sacred Scripture is definitely supreme in the worship experience. We may use other activities, but they are inadequate if we do not include the Word in worship also, for Scripture engraves God's character on the reader's life. Nor should we approach the Scriptures before praying for guidance in their correct interpretation and proper context. Simply knowing the words is not enough—even Satan ably *quoted* Scripture on the Mountain of Temptation. The family should pray that God will give understanding of His plan and enlighten them through the Holy Spirit as they study.

We now suggest that everyone have his own Bible for

worship or that there be a sufficient supply in the worship room. It might avoid confusion if all are the same version. Then everyone can follow along, underlining or memorizing. Discussion is more meaningful if everyone can reread and analyze, chew and digest the passage selected. One reason for not commenting on a text is often that we have already forgotten it.

The family together can dig for truth and at times concentrate on one verse until it is memorized and applied to daily life. (We're cautioned, however, not to search for that which is unusual or curious [see *The Great Controversy,* p. 520].) It often takes mental exertion to open up the Bible. Memorizing isn't easy for many, but it's highly rewarding. Adults may have more difficulty, but children are at the prime age for this.

Going into one home just as the family was ending evening worship was an intriguing experience for us. The parents and teenagers were memorizing the book of James. We asked, "How are you doing?" They responded with laughter, "Not so good at memorizing it since we go so slowly. But we sure do have lots of fun trying to discover what James was saying to us!"

Many children memorize but don't know what the words mean. John tells how as a child he would sing at worship, "Sweet peas, the gift of God's love." It wasn't until later years he discovered that the song was not about flowers but about "peace." Thus an analysis of the text helps, followed by a visualization of the passage. Then the memorizing can begin.

A young man came to our prayer fellowship to share his technique for learning whole chapters of the Bible. His secret was cutting out the verses from an old Bible, pasting them on cards, and then continually rereading them until they began to become a "part of him." All day he carried his cards to reread in spare moments. Upon realizing that he had already automatically memorized large portions, he would then make an effort to memorize the rest. The family can make its own set of cards and practice this technique. Once a week it can go over the passages together. Memorized verses can be used for worships while traveling and/or when Bibles aren't available.

Some frequently memorized portions are Psalms 23, 91, 121; Exodus 20:1-17; Revelation 14:6-12; Matthew 5:1-12; and John 3:16. One acquaintance of ours fondly remembers that in her childhood home the family always repeated Psalm 91 on Friday night. Not only can we put Bible verses to memory but also selections of *The Desire of Ages* dealing with Christ's sufferings. A number of youth and adults are memorizing the last chapter of *The Great Controversy* entitled "The Controversy Ended."

During our husband-and-wife worship time, John and I memorized Psalm 121. Instead of learning it verbatim, we changed it into the first person. Personalizing Scripture makes it more meaningful. Another excellent passage to personalize is Romans 5:1-10 in *The Living Bible*. We made a double-spaced typed copy of it for each one in family worship. While music played in the background, everyone changed the text by crossing out the third person, inserting the first person, and changing the verbs accordingly.

To help the younger children improve their skill in locating different portions of the Bible, you can use "sword drills." One person gives a text, a promise, or a doctrinal verse—and all try to find it quickly. Begin with Bibles closed. The first finder reads the text, and then he or she chooses the next text for the family to track down.

Have you ever tried reading Scripture and having each person draw the story or make symbols for its meaning? A map or diagram of the passage is a most effective way of comprehending a text. It also improves concentration and focuses relationships. When you visualize the story, you can more readily remember it. A good place to start drawing or mapping is the book of Revelation.

A choice Bible reading for teenagers—especially boys—is Proverbs. The book has thirty-one chapters—one for each day of the month. Each person goes through the chapter silently, perhaps underlining parts that particularly appeal to him, with a prayer that God will speak in a special way. Following this, each shares what impressed him most about the chapter. You can also search Proverbs as a word study. Look for all the texts that are on *wise, foolish, righteous, youth,* et cetera.

An important area of Bible study is the doctrines of the church. More and more, parents no longer leave it to the church school teacher or the pastor, but are instructing their own children. Once a week the family can have a doctrinal study, with its members each assigned a different topic. At the Adventist Book Center, you can obtain doctrinal Bible study guides for this worship activity. One parent told what a joy it was to talk about the plan of salvation to her 12-year-old son who accepted Jesus Christ as his personal Saviour for the first time. The Holy Spirit's presence and the beautiful relationship was her mountaintop experience with her son.

The following list of twenty-four suggestions may be helpful in employing the Bible in family worship:

1. Identify character traits of Christ when reading the Gospels. Dialogue on how the family members could develop such admirable characteristics in their own lives.

2. On a Friday or a Sabbath evening, when there is plenty of time, play Bible twenty questions. Identify if it is animal, vegetable, or mineral.

3. Read the narrative stories in *The Living Bible* and develop review questions on them. Try to remember the

facts. Occasionally on Friday night review the fact questions.

4. Pantomime or dramatize Bible stories. Keep an old suitcase full of props and costumes for such occasions. The children may even write scripts and imagine what the Bible characters said. Let a narrator always read what Jesus said. Avoid letting any of the children be a Judas.

5. Search the Scriptures for texts about fathers, mothers, husbands, wives, children, youth, or the aged. Choose a night when you read the texts for the mother and have each person affirm her on that night.

6. Read a chapter of the Bible together. Then privately write feelings about some portion of it. Each is to visualize himself doing what God commands and then make plans to act upon His instruction the next day.

7. Select a passage from the Bible to read which relates to Christ in the Gospels, such as John 15:1-15; Luke 4:7-14, et cetera. Discuss the plot and the scene. Each is to choose a verse from the passage and share why it is meaningful. Personalize the message of Jesus as though He were speaking. Have each write how he feels about Jesus saying this to him. After jotting down the feelings, share them with the family.

8. Have a red-letter-edition Bible. Let the young child who is just learning to read, read the words in red while other individuals read the text in black.

9. In each person's worship Bible underline all doctrinal texts in green. Later make a chain reference by topics. After they have underlined basic doctrines, assign each family member to take the rest through a doctrinal study.

10. Underline all promises using a blue pen. Then take time to memorize the texts and where they are found in the Bible. Start in Matthew, learn all the promises in this book, and then proceed to Mark. You

can also do the same thing with the doctrinal texts. Continue book by book.

11. Make a collection of Bible promises and identify whether the promises are for guidance, help, healing, speaking, et cetera. Use at worship when needed by any family member.

12. Do a thorough biographical study on characters of the Bible and evaluate God's dealings in their lives. Study and list cause and effect of choices made by them.

13. Study by topics using the concordance as help. Good topic words can be wisdom, Holy Spirit, lead, guide, peace, hope, and faith.

14. Take the family through the Voice of Prophecy or Faith for Today Bible study courses.

15. Assign a text for the family to analyze. Sometime during the day each person will write about what the text is saying to him and share it at evening worship.

16. Memorize the Creation week events and discuss the topic of evolution.

17. Teach the family how to use footnotes in the Bible or the marginal helps.

18. Read orally parts of Job, Isaiah, and Psalms as examples of Bible poetry. Enjoy the beauty of the literary style.

19. Learn the books of the Bible by making a game of it.

20. Read to find the plan of salvation. Record the texts. Then have each person practice at some worship time how he would guide someone else to accept Jesus Christ as his personal Saviour.

21. Study Bible maps so stories will become more meaningful.

22. Make an imaginary trip to the Middle East. Each person can share what certain places were like—Bethany, Jerusalem, Nazareth, Jericho.

23. Read Joel and Malachi. Discuss which things

mentioned there will happen in the last days.

24. Have children who are starting school practice reading from Genesis 1. Most of the words are one syllable, and the repetition makes it an ideal portion of the Bible to use as a reading primer.

The Use of Ellen White Books in Family Worship

How fortunate we Adventists are to have such beautiful insights on the Bible through the pen of Ellen White. While her writings are not to supersede the Bible, they are our spiritual telescope. They do not create new light, but magnify the light already present in the Bible. The Bible should be our great sourcebook for family worship. It is an unfailing chart which directs and guides us. In addition, or for a change, we refer to the writings of Ellen White as commentary on the Bible.

In our family worships, we try not to use her writings to hammer home some particular point. They are basically not "no-no" books, and we try not to present them so to our sons. We believe it is one reason why they appreciate the books and now study them on their own. If we must correct the children regarding some improper course of action, let's deal with the problem faithfully, but not hammer our family with hard statements from Ellen G. White, oftentimes taken out of their context of encouragement and concern.

The story is told of a man who quoted profusely from Ellen White for his family worship, usually from the specific book he read that month. He referred to it as his "Book of the Month Club." The children, however, called it the "Club of the Month Book"! Let's work with the priceless materials from a positive viewpoint and not equate them in the minds of the children with negative lambasting.

The following list of twenty suggestions may be helpful in planning worships using the writings of Ellen

White as resources:

1. Read about the Biblical prophets and imagine what it would have been like to have possessed the prophetic gift.

2. Study the Bible tests of a true prophet.

3. Read a devotional book such as *The Story of Redemption* together as a family, with each person having his copy of the same book.

4. Make a collection of promises found in the Bible and Spirit of Prophecy. Each time someone finds a promise, record it in the Family Promise Book.

5. Use the *Comprehensive Index to the Writings of Ellen G. White* to find selections on topics such as happiness, compassion, salvation, or guidance.

6. Read on stewardship and then have the family decide if they would like to start a self-denial box for missionary activities.

7. Father or mother might go through *The Story of Redemption* for personal devotion to see what it says about angels. Then in a series of worships read the angel stories from this book to the family. Follow up with discussion on how angels are part of the individual Christian's family life.

8. Study the life of Ellen G. White. Find stories of interesting incidents and experiences.

9. Begin a "Fruits of the Spirit" notebook prepared by the family by looking up in indexes the topics of love, joy, peace, et cetera, and recording choice quotes.

10. Take *The Desire of Ages* and read the chapters "As a Child" and "Days of Conflict," first identifying the character traits of Christ as a child and then as a youth. Make a check list for the family and decide which traits the family would like to work toward.

11. On older children's birthdays read from letters Ellen White wrote to her children on their birthdays.

12. On Thursday evening or Friday morning read for

worship instruction concerning Sabbath preparation.

13. On Sabbath morning read concerning how to keep the Sabbath holy. Put some information into a Family Worship Book and add to it frequently and reread for Sabbath worships.

14. Have each family member research in Ellen White's books on one of the Ten Commandments. Have them share what they mean at worship time until the family has covered all the commandments. Put the results into Family Worship Notebook.

15. Choose a choice promise from one of Ellen White's books on which the family will dialogue by analyzing words, visualizing what the passage says, and deciding how each will put into actual practice the message of God for the day. Memorize and include in the Family Worship Notebook.

16. Let different family members select a specific character trait of God that they would like to possess and research it in the writings of Ellen White. Pray that the Holy Spirit will help them to develop the trait.

17. Have children read about the early life of Ellen White from *Early Writings.*

18. Read the first vision of Ellen White found in *Early Writings,* pages 14-20. Have family respond with their imagination and visualization of what they saw in their minds as they read the story. (This could be in a series.)

19. Read narratives from the Conflict of the Ages Series with your teenagers at evening worships, each one having a copy of the books.

20. Topics the family can study with aid of the index to the writings of Ellen White are: courage, sympathy, decisions, disposition, courtesy, thinking, mind, giving, habits, thankfulness, usefulness, wisdom, unselfishness, trials, study, self-respect, and patience. Combine her statements with Bible texts.

Creative Altar Suggestions

"Let there be singing in the home, of songs that are sweet and pure, and there will be fewer words of censure and more of cheerfulness and hope and joy."— Education, *p. 168.*

Music in Family Worship

Normal, healthy children are, on occasion, restless and uncooperative during family worship. If you knew of something to help them be a little sweeter and happier, of course you would want to use it! Music can answer this need.

"Song has a wonderful power. It has power to subdue rude and uncultivated natures; power to quicken thought and to awaken sympathy, to promote harmony of action, and to banish the gloom and foreboding that destroy courage and weaken effort."—*Education,* p. 168.

When the Lord led His children through an experience of frustration, discouragement, and trial—their wilderness journey—He encouraged them through music. After the Ten Commandments had echoed from the majesty of Sinai, they were not just tucked away into the ark. By God's own directive, the Israelites made them into song.

Some they sang as the great company traveled in the wilderness. They must have had a distinctive slow beat that everyone could keep time to. Left, right, left, right, "I *am* the *Lord* your *God* who *brought* you *out* of *E*-gypt." Musical instruments accompanied them, somewhat like the horns and drums in a high school parade, and the people sang in time as they trudged the long, hot miles. Far out over the lonely desert rang the promises, commandments, and past blessings of God.

"Thus their thoughts were uplifted from the trials and difficulties of the way, the restless, turbulent spirit was soothed and calmed, . . . and faith was strengthened."—*Education,* p. 39.

During His childhood, youth, and ministry, Jesus loved to sing. "With songs of thanksgiving He [Jesus] cheered His hours of labor and brought heaven's gladness to the toilworn and disheartened."—*Ministry of Healing,* p. 52.

As the children learn songs in worship they build a reservoir of power to use in work and play as well as for times of praise or discouragement. Christ was also our example in this. "The early morning often found Him in some secluded place, meditating, searching the Scriptures, or in prayer. With the voice of singing He welcomed the morning light."—*Ibid.*

Song was a vital part of the morning and evening worship of our early Adventist believers, producing both calm and joy. Our pioneers sang everywhere they went—as they went about their daily tasks and while riding their horse-drawn carriages to their meetings. They sang with electrifying power at their song services.

"Whenever James and Ellen White found a group of gloomy, depressed Adventists, Elder White would suggest to his wife, 'Come Ellen, let's sing for them.' The two would stand and sing, and as their sweetly blended voices bore a message of cheer to weary hearts, it seemed as if the channels of heavenly peace were opened afresh."—Ella White Robinson, "Beloved Hymns of Ellen White," record jacket.

The Whites always sang for morning and evening worship. William White, a son, recorded one such experience: "At seven o'clock all assembled in the parlor for morning worship. Father would read an appropriate scripture, with comments, and then lead in the morning song of praise or supplication, in which all joined. The hymn most frequently used was:

'Lord, in the morning Thou shalt hear
My voice ascending high;
To Thee will I direct my prayer,
To Thee lift up mine eye.'

"This or some other song of a somewhat similar character was sung with hearty vigor, and then father prayed."—W. C. White, "Sketches and Memories of James and Ellen G. White," *Review and Herald,* Feb. 13, 1936.

The Bible makes it clear that song should be a part of morning and evening worship. "It is a good thing to give thanks unto the Lord, and to sing praises unto thy name, O most High: to shew forth thy lovingkindness in the morning, and thy faithfulness every night" (Ps. 92:1, 2).

The Whites memorized hymns. Then they would go around the circle to see if each one knew the words.

The family might enjoy singing one of the favorites used by Ellen White in her family worships. She particularly favored the hymn "Jesus, Lover of My Soul." Other songs often sung in the White home included "O Worship the Lord," "We Speak of the Realms," "I Heard the Voice of Jesus Say," and "I Will Never Leave Thee."

One father confided that his teenagers weren't very joyful during worship. But he discovered that when they participated by playing the piano or clarinet, they seemed to enter into the spirit of worship and found it a more pleasant experience. The power in sacred song can enhance the family's spiritual hour.

A young minister decided to help his children tie home worship with Sabbath church worship. Along with having the children find the Scripture reading texts for the next service, he had them learn the songs that were to be used as well. Thus the church service became more meaningful to his family.

One mother mentioned how her son, who had a good singing voice, would entertain himself for long periods by playing and singing Bible verses. The whole family might try to learn and sing different verses each evening so as to reinforce their Bible learning. The Scriptures will become indelibly inscribed on the memory, a treasure never to be forgotten. (Your children's Sabbath school memory verse song tapes are available at the Adventist Book Center.)*

One family copied all the Bible verses set to music on cards, and when it was a member's time to choose a song for worship, he would pull a card from the stack. Even if it's just a verse or a chorus, the singing of short selections of the Bible set to music enhances any worship experience.

When our son returned home from being a junior camp counselor, he suggested we spend more time singing in worship as they had done at camp. Responding to his suggestion, we bought enough worship songbooks for each of us to enjoy his own. Especially on Friday night our family enjoys sharing a number of songs. During the early teen years there often occurs a period when boys dislike singing, but fortunately most young men outgrow that stage.

A memorized song goes wherever the learner does. When traveling, we don't always have access to songbooks, but if we have memorized songs, we'll still be able to enjoy singing together. We know one couple

---

***Sing the Word* is a songbook and tape of Bible verses set to music that our family enjoys. Carolyn Bisel and Dan Klein compiled and edited it, and it also is available from your Adventist Book Center. Also available are "Singing Sampler," a cassette with voice and accompaniement, and "Duo Piano," two cassettes that include the performance of all songs listed in the songbook with accompaniment only.

who are preparing for a time when Bibles and hymnals might possibly be taken away. While they walk a distance of several miles to school and work, they memorize new songs. Through the summer dust or winter snow, they walk, learn, and sing hundreds of verses which they wouldn't otherwise know.

Parents can prepare a loose-leaf family hymnal for each member of the family, containing the particular hymns the family is trying to memorize. Some families reward each child who masters the words of a song within a week's time. Recorded songs played in worship often help us commit the words to memory. In our family we traditionally played one record to awaken the family on Sabbath morning and we had another for bedtime. When Wes came home from boarding academy, he wanted us to play the traditional record. To him it had become the symbol of family evening prayer.

Some families show a slide presentation of nature scenes coordinated with appropriate hymns. The family may make their own slides and choose songs to accompany them. One or more family members can locate appropriate script material, and they can incorporate musical recordings or play an instrument themselves. This could be a special program for a Friday night worship.

A bottle orchestra can be a delight. Fill bottles with various amounts of water. You make the tone by striking the bottles with a hard object. The children could spend some time preparing these bottles to have them ready for worship time. Only our own imaginations will limit creative musical worship!

Take a family survey and determine the top ten favorite hymns of your family. Sing them once a week during the Sabbath celebration. As interests change, revise the list.

Other families write their own worship songs. Just as

many families have a coat of arms which represents characteristics about them, why not write a song about your family and its spiritual growth? If you don't have sufficient talent for composing the music as well, the family could pick a familiar hymn and write new lyrics about themselves. Remember, creativity and worship go together. As we bring out the creative in us, we are better able to honor the Creator.

Here are other hints for using music in the family: keep copies of the words of new songs at different places in the house, so that during a spare moment family members can learn a few lines. Later the family can rehearse together during worship. While the children are still young, study the types of music appropriate for a Christian family to listen to—before the evil one occupies the ground. The *Comprehensive Index to the Writings of Ellen G. White* is a helpful reference guide. Play beautiful, sacred classical music to sensitize the taste of the children. If we preoccupy the ground with the best, our families will have no desire or room for the inferior.

Satan also employs music to emphasize certain thoughts in our minds. Why not use it, then, to reinforce sacred thoughts and glorify God by songs of praise? Sacred music can bring peace and joy into family worship, drawing us to God. It helps us memorize the truths of God more easily and can be as powerful as prayer. Music encourages us throughout the day and fortifies the mind with spiritual truth. Our sacred singing on this earth is a rehearsal for the occasion when we will join the redeemed and the angels at the great coronation of our Saviour as they burst forth with the Song of Moses and the Lamb.

Prayer and Praise as Worship

The school of the prophets taught the young men how to pray. The disciples learned how to pray from

Jesus. They requested of Him, "Teach us to pray."

The families that have a close walk with the Lord are those that have studied the science of prayer and the conditions of answered prayer. Prayer for the infants leads to the tiny tot sentence prayers, repeating parent prayer phrases, and then moves to the child's original prayers. With each stage of development, the prayers can become more advanced and powerful. But admit, we must, that at times the child has greater faith than the adult.

How wonderful it is when the child early learns to pray. While John learned as an infant to pray, I didn't pray until I opened a new chapter of my life in a Christian college and found myself forced into a prayer group by a worship requirement.

Many a husband would like to conduct worship in the home but is uncomfortable about praying in front of others. That is why it is so essential to start early.

Praise is a part of prayer and is a form of worship. We may use the praise texts in the Bible as prayer for both our personal and family devotions.

More Prayer and Praise Family Altar Suggestions

1. Study to find God's conditions for answering prayer.

2. Have topic prayers. Every person prays about some topic, being very specific. For example, in the first round of prayer, everyone prays about the Holy Spirit working in his life. Next every participant prays again about a person who may be in need of God's guidance. A third round might be of praise and faith that God has answered the prayers.

3. Start a very specific prayer list with only five things on it. Add a new item when one of the prayers is answered. Choose requests wisely so that children will not become discouraged.

4. Have each person find a praise text with which to start worship.

5. Make a list of praise terms found in David's psalms.

6. When you have small children, have a family hug and kiss after prayer.

7. Discuss how to pray and for what to pray.

8. Claim promises with prayer requests.

9. Keep in sight of all (on refrigerator or bathroom mirror) special prayer requests for the day.

10. Thank God for answered prayer before it is answered.

11. Explain the reason for praying in Jesus' name.

12. Sing prayers such as "If I Have Wounded Any Soul Today" or "Saviour, Like a Shepherd Lead Us."

13. Encourage sending spontaneous prayers throughout the day for family members.

14. Hold hands and kneel facing each other, making an altar while praying. Avoid not facing each other while praying.

15. Invite God's presence in worship by a short invocation.

16. Touch the head of the person the rest of the family is praying for.

17. Pray silently on occasion.

18. Use a text prayer, such as "Let the words of my mouth, and the meditation of my heart . . . "

19. Concentrate on a different prayer project each day of the week.

20. Make a special prayer log book in which you list on a given date your special needs and requests. Next write in those promises you will claim in regard to the requests. As the problems are solved and your prayers answered, write in red after the request the date and way God answered.

21. Pray for those who send you Christmas cards.

Take one Christmas card each day and pray throughout the day for that individual. Then write the person, reporting that you prayed for him in a special way. Continue throughout the year until you have prayed for every card sender.

22. Choose a different person each week to pray for specifically, like a missionary friend, a student, a neighbor, an invalid, or someone soliciting prayers. Write the person, telling him of your prayers in his behalf.

23. Keep a record of answered prayers in a miracle book.

24. Have a special prayer list for Sabbath morning or Friday night worship. At the beginning of a new year start a fresh list and put the old one in a prayer book, rededicating each person to the Lord.

25. Read letters from relatives and then pray for those individuals.

26. Have a prayer walk. While walking, talk to God for twenty to twenty-five minutes. This can make one healthier physically and spiritually.

27. Pray that God will help in the preparation of worship topics.

Keeping the Fires Burning

"All who consecrate soul, body, and spirit to God will be constantly receiving a new endowment of physical and mental power. The inexhaustible supplies of heaven are at their command."—The Desire of Ages, *p. 827.*

It Isn't Easy

Being a parent isn't a popularity contest. It isn't always easy to hold family worships that will please everyone, particularly the upper teens. TV and other media are hard to compete with. One 19-year-old college student announced to his father that he had personal worship, worship at his work, and at the start of his classes, and he didn't want to have to attend family worship anymore. His wise father didn't debate or become defensive. He said, "Son, your last name is Miller. There are certain characteristics or traditions of the Miller family—things that we just always do together. The Millers go to church on Sabbath morning, we have the custom of eating at least one meal a day all together, and we have a short worship morning and evening recognizing that Jesus is Lord of the Miller family and asking His help in our family relationships. We're proud to have you as a member of the Miller family, and we expect to have your support in family worship." The young man continued to attend family worship. Billy Miller will soon graduate from college. As he goes out into life to establish a home of his own, he will take with him a tradition that the family altar is important and one not to dispense with lightly. What finer legacy could his father have given him?

A seminary student told how hard he studied for a particular exam, depriving his wife and children of his time and skipping his worship with them. His anxiety level was very high and he felt he could take no time off for anything else. Just before the exam he rushed out the door of the house without saying goodbye or kissing his wife and children. As he was driving over to the seminary class, he realized what he was doing and decided that he didn't like it. Arriving a few minutes early he went to the professor and told him his problem. He said, "This is not my lifestyle, and I abhor it, and I'm not going to subject my family to this kind of behavior." Then he asked to be excused from the test and went home. When he got there he knocked on the door and beamed as his surprised wife greeted him. After explaining what had happened, they had their devotional and family worship with their little children. Then the four of them took off for a family day together. Were their priorities right?

Bobbie, a handsome, suntanned surfer and football player told us his story in Hawaii. He and his wife had had a new experience with the Lord and knew that the only way to keep a close relationship with Jesus Christ was through their devotions and family worship. On a particular day it was time for work, but for some reason they still had not had worship. Although Bobbie left in a rush, he only got as far as his car. Then, realizing that his priorities were incorrect, he told us, "I decided I'm going back into the house, and my wife and I will have worship even if I'm late to work thirty minutes."

On that very day, Bobbie, an electrician, reported to a certain job where it was necessary to climb a pole to a high-tension line. The job assigned was a dangerous one due to the complexity of the high-voltage wires. When he was already on the pole he realized that he was not protected by some of the safety equipment that he normally used, but he went ahead anyway, trying to be careful. As he was working, suddenly he touched a live wire. Sparks went flying and so did Bobbie. The current passed through his body and left a large burn in the arch of his foot. Another worker had a similar experience with the same voltage, but he didn't live to tell the story. Bobbie's friends witnessed the accident in amazement and disbelief. "It's just because you are so physically fit and healthy that you aren't dead!" they reasoned. But Bobbie testified, "The living God was watching over me." That evening he and his wife praised the Lord in their worship for sparing his life. They felt that it was an angel impressing him to go back into the house that morning where he and his wife had prayed for divine protection.

My Dream—A Worship Room

We all like to do a little daydreaming. One of ours has been to have a home chapel totally dedicated to the worship of Jehovah. Wouldn't it be delightful to have a home sanctuary exclusively for family and individual worship—a room sufficiently soundproof to keep the outside distracting noises away, properly ventilated and decorated attractively with indirect lights, a scenic or Biblical mural lining the wall, and green plants accenting the atmosphere? The worship room might open onto a patio with ferns and flowers and an outdoor bench for meditating. Of course, inside the little chapel would have to be soft carpets for kneeling and a comfortable sofa and chairs. A stereo would enhance the atmosphere with appropriate tapes and records to play, and a piano or organ for music lovers. A neatly organized library standing against the wall would be advantageous, with a desk for writing. It's just a dream, and too costly for most to build, but how nice it would be, don't you agree?

But now we use many different places for worship in our home. Ellen White writes about having worship at the breakfast table or at the fireside. It could be in the child's bedroom or on the lawn in the summertime. When our boys were younger and had inexhaustible energy, we would spend a day out in nature, ending it with worship in a forest or beside a stream. No matter where we are, God's presence is at our family altar.

On one such Sabbath day we found ourselves on the sandy shores of Lake Michigan at sunset. While Curley Dog raced from one person to another in pure ecstasy, we sat down on a secluded sand dune and lifted our voices in the song "Day Is Dying in the West." I recall that as we watched the sun sink into the horizon of Lake Michigan, our family sat praising the Lord for His blessings. We were thankful for skateboards, good jobs, warm homes, soft pillows, water for bathing, Curley Dog, good health, appetites (about this time the sons were good and hungry), Linketts, friends, Jesus' love, bikes, Grandma who lives with us and prays for us, angels to help us, and the list went on and on until twilight turned into darkness. Reluctantly we departed, leaving behind God's altar in its beauty, but recording the special moment in our life's notebook of memories.

More General Family Altar Suggestions

1. Read a continuous story suitable for all age levels.
2. Conduct family council once a week to discuss projects, goals, and routines (after a short worship).
3. Discuss sex education for worship as part of God's beautiful plan for humankind.
4. Write appreciation notes to family members once a month.
5. Worship with some invalid friend of the family.
6. Prepare a "thankful list' with each family member contributing.

7. Practice the presence of Christ in worship.

8. Ask for forgiveness for specific mistakes of the day.

9. Conduct worship service in nature by a stream, the ocean, the sand dunes, or in the woods.

10. Use nature items for spiritual object lessons. Play a Bible game made up by the family or use a purchased game such as The Ungame or Social Security.

11. Conduct worship in different family members' bedrooms.

12. Practice light fasting during the times of crucial family decisions.

13. For special birthday worships tell the story of birth circumstances and discuss personal goals for the new year of life.

14. Dedicate new babies to God during worship.

15. Experience a candlelight or fireplace worship on Friday nights.

16. Set an extra plate at the Christmas table and invite the heavenly Guest to worship with the family. Perhaps invite in an aged, homeless, or ill person to sit at that place, representing Jesus.

17. Play a sing-along record for worship.

18. Have doctrinal quizzes.

19. Use flannel storyboards or black light.

20. Have all family members write their opinions and feelings on a spiritual issue.

21. Celebrate a special occasion like a baptism (second birth), anniversary, finishing the eighth or twelfth grade.

22. Read books about marriage such as *I Married You, I Loved a Girl,* or *Communication Key to Your Marriage* (for teens and parents).

23. Start worship by having each person state what good things happened to him/her during the day.

24. Write a letter to God like that to a friend.

25. Set a specific time for worship and try to keep to it.

26. Invite neighbors to have worship with your family on a certain day.

27. Indicate that worship time has arrived by playing the piano, playing a certain tape or record, ringing a soft bell, et cetera.

28. Celebrate an agape feast just for the family, thanking God for His blessings. Have white candles and an Eden diet of just fresh fruits, nuts, and bread. Avoid general conversation. Spend the time talking of God's goodness, sharing texts, and giving testimonies of faith and hope.

29. Have early worship with tiny tots as soon as you have dressed them for bed.

30. Have a special storybook for tiny tots that they bring for their part of the worship time.

31. Adapt topics to language of the young child.

32. Study the Sabbath school lesson silently and then all share the meaningful parts. Have Sabbath school lesson for tiny tots separate from that of the older children.

33. Recount important episodes in the family history and how God guided in conversion and important decisions of ancestors.

34. Read the yearly Morning Watch books—adult or youth.

35. Have a *needs* worship. Each participant writes down two or three felt needs on a card. Next read them. Go around the circle with each contributing a promise which could help meet someone's needs. Then kneel for prayer. Person A prays for needs of B, B prays for C, and C prays for needs of A.

36. Have a worship corner for tiny tots that has a flannelgraph board, pictures of Jesus, religious coloring books, and nature objects for lessons. Children can

rehearse daily story using flannel pictures during the day. At evening worship they tell the stories to mother and dad.

37. On separate cards make a list of people to pray for. At every meal pull a card and pray for that person.

38. Invite new church members to have worship with the family.

39. Leave a scripture or devotional thought on the breakfast table for late risers.

40. Start Friday evening by lighting a candle so children will know when the Sabbath begins.

Heart-turning and -tuning

" 'Behold, I will send you Elijah the prophet
Before the coming of the great and dreadful day of the Lord.
And he will turn
The hearts of the fathers to the children,
And the hearts of the children to their fathers' "
(Mal. 4:5, 6, N.K.J.V.).

Has your heart ever fluttered, skipped a beat, or pounded a bit when you saw someone you loved? Perhaps the days of teenage romance come to our minds. That love was a total response to someone special. God is in the business of making that happen today—between spouses and between parents and children. There are many ways it can occur. Let's consider two of the most important ones: celebrations and family traditions.

Celebration

Wes had a case of the blues. His active lifestyle and involvement in several sports had come to an abrupt end. One power dive on the skateboard had changed it all. He had lost his balance and had shattered his wrist. The splint and sling seemed like prison to him. Millie and I were feeling financially pinched ourselves with "too much month left at the end of the money." The solution to our depressions was to *celebrate,* and we knew it would have to be homemade. The whole family got into the mood for this surprise event. As Wes entered the garage he encountered a large sign tacked to a sawhorse: "You are invited to an important event! Follow the trail for further information." The "trail" consisted of some surplus sticky wrapping tape. The trail had several stops and led to his room. Then Dad asked him to go out to the mailbox and check if there was any mail for Grandma. At the box he found an envelope twenty-four by thirty-six inches. The "stamp" was a picture of a famous person—a photograph of Wes! He came back into the house, somewhat stunned, and opened the envelope. The booklet chronicled important events of his life complete with cartoons. It contained messages from every member of the family, adding up to "Happy Eighteenth Birthday." Taped to the card was a $15 check that helped to lift his spirit. The messages were affirmation of his person and expressed confidence that God had called him for an important purpose and work. Back in the kitchen we served "poverty cake"—brownies with candles on them. Then Dad took out the diary of eighteen years ago and read the account of Wes's birth. He dramatically recounted how he had been out on a missionary trip and had rushed from an evening meeting in the backcountry of Chile to get to the clinic in time for his son's 4:00 A.M. birth. In prayer we closed worship rededicating Wes and the rest of the family to God. It was a fun birthday celebration that we treasure in our storehouse of memories. We enjoyed it as parents and it affirmed Wes in his personhood as someone special.

It's fun to celebrate spiritual occasions as well. Our sons came to the breakfast table, sat down, and a quizzical look spread over their faces. Underneath each of their plates was a colorful homemade placemat that declared, "Congratulations on your special day! Do you know what happened on this date?" John looked at Wes, and he stared back. Puzzled, John said, "It's not my birthday. It's not your birthday. What's all the celebration about?"

"December 5 . . . h'mm . . ."

"I know. It's our baptismal date!"

Yes, five years before, our sons had been baptized together. It was their spiritual birthday. We passed the original baptismal certificates which they had signed, and pictures of the occasion around the table. Then we read an appropriate Bible passage and said warm words of thankfulness for how they had grown in the Lord over the past five years. After a prayer of rededication, Mom served a special breakfast with some of their favorite goodies. Nobody complained that morning worship bored them that day!

There are many ways of celebrating life. In our family, given half an excuse, we are always ready to celebrate. Celebration puts zest into the worship experience. The memories made strengthen our family relationships and turn our hearts to one another.

Building Family Traditions

When certain expressions or celebrations are habitually repeated, they become family traditions. They are powerful transmitters of religious heritage.

Paul and I attended church school together. Then our family moved away and we lost contact. Thirty-five years later our paths crossed again and we invited him home for a fellowship meal to remember old times. I knew that Paul had had some rough spiritual times in childhood and I was surprised to learn that he now held an important position in our worldwide church. After supper we dusted off an old school yearbook. Several schoolmates were dead, many were divorced, and sadly an amazing number had lost their walk with the Lord.

"Paul," I asked him, "to what do you attribute your strength and faithfulness in the Christian lifestyle?"

He thought a bit. "Well, John, I've had my ups and downs, but there was one thing I could never forget in life. Every time I left home my loving mother was there.

She would put her hand on my shoulder as I was leaving the house and tenderly say in her broken English, 'Son, go vith Got.' Those words ringing in my ears had a strong magnetic pull. I always felt that God's presence was with me."

In many homes family worship has become a settled part of the family tradition. Although children may leave the nest, they know at the hour of the morning and evening sacrifice exactly what mom and dad are doing. Liz was a young lady who had spiritually rebelled. But strange heart-tugs kept coming back into her memories. When she awakened in the morning, her thoughts would wander back to home. What were her mom and dad doing? She would glance at the clock and know that they were just finishing their personal devotions, and she could visualize them going to the living room for family worship just like they did when she was a child. They would sing, read the Bible out loud, and pray together. Liz didn't keep the Sabbath, but when the sacred hours arrived she would recall Sabbath at home. As the twilight gathered on Friday evening, her mom would play "Day Is Dying in the West," and the family would join in song together. Pecan rolls made Friday night supper special. The kitchen would be sparkling clean, with Sabbath dinner all prepared and ready to pop in the oven when they came home from church. She remembered her mother's hurt look after one of the confrontations when she as a teenager had declared independence from home and from the church. Often sleep would not come in the night as she realized the heartache of her parents who loved her so but were willing to let her go. Her unkindness had been repaid with kindness. The strange feelings in her heart toward them and Christ were compelling. The memories of what home stood for, inspired by the Spirit of God, helped to convict her. One day she had to surrender—"Here am I,

Lord," she yielded at last. "I'm Yours. You are the victor!"

Family Covenant Renewal

Family covenant renewal is another way to tune hearts to God and each other. From time to time we all need to be confronted with a choice and to make or to renew a commitment regarding some of life's meaningful values. We can plan a commitment service that will be unforgettable. One of our family covenants, however, was not scheduled, but happened under unforgettable circumstances.

Millie and I had been married only a short time. (My first wife had passed away.) It was vacation time, and we had looked forward to getting out with the family to Colorado. We were still adapting to each other, and the boys were adjusting to their new mother and she to them.

We headed west toward the Rocky Mountains. But with four people cooped up hour after hour in a little car, the children were getting on our nerves and we on theirs. In addition, we were trying to write a book about marriage commitment, and at every campsite we would write a few more pages. By now everybody was completely frustrated.

It happened at Ouray, Colorado. We were at the lovely Amphitheater Campground where God and nature seem to meet. John and Wes enjoyed the hang-gliding events at nearby Telluride, and Wes got his thrills skateboarding over a mile down the hill to the picturesque town below. I still remember the day. Although it was a beautiful morning, the family wasn't speaking to one another. Can you imagine what day of the week it was? It was Sabbath. Satan seems to work a little harder at making people angry with one another on that day.

This particular morning, Millie had *had it*. She was about ready to turn in her "mother button." Thinking it might help, I asked the family to go for a hike and have our own worship service out on the trail. We climbed up to a turn in the pathway and could see the camp far below and the mountains in the distance. When it began to rain, we stopped under a large pine tree and sat on a log. There we began to evaluate our family and our problems. Without negative emotions we began to communicate. After a bit, I said, "We all really have the same goals. Why don't we join hands in a circle and make a covenant with God to support one another and determine to help one another?"

While the rain fell on our little circle, the peace of the Holy Spirit also showered on us. I prayed. Millie prayed that God would help her to be a good mother. My son John prayed that God would help us polish up the rough places in our lives. Wes thanked God that we had an opportunity to understand one another better. The boys then ran down the mountain, and I asked, "Millie, do you think that God is going to answer our prayers?"

"Yes," she answered, "I do."

Recently, speaking appointments took us to the West Coast. As we were winging our way back toward home in Berrien Springs, Michigan, the captain's voice came over the public-address system. "On the right side of the aircraft you have an excellent view of Telluride, Colorado." My eyes followed the road from the town winding through the canyons to Ouray some thirty miles away. I could see the majestic ridges above the Amphitheater Campground, and somewhere down there at a bend in the trail under a pine tree was a sacred spot in the history of the Youngberg family. Over a decade had passed. We have had our trials and misunderstandings as any four people who live in close proximity are bound to have. But beneath, there is something solid and unchanging—a covenant, a pact with God and one another that we are committed to His plan for our lives and want to support one another.

It was the Sabbath afternoon previous to John junior's graduation from college. The doorbell rang, and to his surprise in walked his major professor who had meant more to his career than anyone else at college. A few minutes later the doorbell rang again and in walked the president and executive director of Maranatha Flights International, men who directed the organization John worked for and who had inspired him toward a life of service. Obviously something was up. We helped 92-year-old Grandma up from her downstairs apartment, and we all loaded into several cars and headed for the cemetery.

All the immediate family and the most significant others in John's life gathered around the grave of his mother who had died twelve years before. Her tombstone would be a silent witness to this covenant ceremony. As father of the family, I took out a document that I had spent hours preparing. It recounted his early life and crucial moments of decision. It recalled his baptism and his solemn choice to follow Jesus. And it spoke of his bent toward construction, stirring up the realization that the greatest and most long-lasting building that he was rearing was his own character. He thought of the tens of thousands of prayers that his mother Bonnie had prayed for him. The memories admonished him to be faithful to God, to the family, and to himself.

Next each significant person present spoke words of affirmation. Millie reminded him that she had now been a part of his life for as long a time as his first mother had. Wes gave his brotherly admonition. His academic and career supervisors gave support and challenge. When all had finished, we asked him for a statement of his response. After he publicly rededicated his life to do the will of God and to service for mankind, we joined hands in one circle around his mother's tombstone. Grandma sealed the covenant with a prayer that this grandson with whom she had been almost all of his 24 years might be faithful, and that all of us might gather again in an unbroken circle in God's eternal home. We treasure the memory of that celebration and covenant, particularly since Grandma now rests a few feet from Bonnie awaiting the day of which she prayed. She is gone, but we thank God that younger hands have accepted the torch.

In Old Testament times God instructed that His people should periodically renew the covenant in an impressive ceremony. The book of Deuteronomy records one such occasion. At the end of the ceremony the people repeated the blessings and the curses, and then Moses called heaven and earth as witnesses while he challenged them to choose between life and death (see Deut. 30:15, 19). Every seven years the covenant document was to be read again at the Feast of Tabernacles. A generation later Joshua solemnly renewed the covenant before his death. He challenged the people, "Choose you this day whom ye will serve; . . . but as for me and my house, we will serve the Lord" (Joshua 24:15). In the times of Hezekiah, Josiah, and Ezra, Israel's leaders reread the Book of the Law (Deuteronomy) to the people and added God's more recent saving acts to the list. Thus the covenant was renewed. It is a matter of historical record that a great revival and reformation accompanied each of the occasions. Today parents should recount to children God's saving acts in their lives, and invite them to join in a solemn covenant of faithfulness to God and one another.

Tuning the Strings

A family is like a violin that the Master took. He drew His bow across one string and found it too shrill. Trying another, He discovered it too flat. Another sounded fine by itself, but it was still out of pitch. One was too loose and needed tightening. The Master paused and sounded a true note on His pitch pipe, then He began to tune the strings. He tightened here a little, loosened there. Not expecting every string to sound just the same, He drew His bow again and again until all blended together in harmonious music.

The Elijah message of today is turning hearts of family members to one another, and it is *tuning hearts* so that the family may blend in beautiful harmony. Some parents have given their instrument to another master who is playing his own discordant notes and causing confusion. Some are trying to let God play some notes and Satan others. To them the Elijah message says, "How long will you go limping between two opinions? If Jehovah is God, worship Him, or if Baal is your choice, worship him." Family members must be called back to a clear note—God's law—and then adjust and tune their lives accordingly. The high places are to be brought down, and the low places are to be raised. Some family members are too rasping; they must be mellowed. Others hang so loose they need to allow the Master to stretch and discipline them.

The curtain is opening. Like a live violin you are on center stage. Two masters vie for control of your strings. A world and a universe wait breathlessly to see who will play the notes. Shall we not give our families into the nail-pierced hands of the loving Master to tune our strings—that men and angels might hear rapturous music—every string different but blended in beautiful harmony?